SASSY DOG PRODUCTIONS INC.

PASSING DOWN YOUR SUCCESS

How to Prepare Your Family and Business for the First Transition

TAMMY BUSS

CONTENTS

INTRODUCTION   1

1. WHAT DO YOU WANT AND HOW ARE YOU GETTING THERE?   11

2. THE IMPORTANCE OF FAMILY AND BUSINESS COMMUNICATION   23

3. THE BUSINESS CIRCLE   41

4. THE OWNERSHIP CIRCLE   51

5. THE FAMILY CIRCLE   63

6. THE FAMILY MEETING   73

7. START PREPARING YOUR BUSINESS FOR SUCCESSION TODAY   93

CONCLUSION   109

APPENDIX   113

INTRODUCTION

"The only place success comes before work is in the dictionary."
—Vince Lombardi, Hall of Fame American Football Coach

When I started out in business, I was young and like so many founders didn't really know what I was doing. To me I was just making a living. I ended up growing a business and many years later had to plan for selling and/or transitioning out.

Even though my husband and I worked together, in separate sides of the business, I still didn't think of it as a family business. Then it hit me when our son joined the business, after my husband retired. *Holy crap, I actually have a family business. How do I transition this now?* I realized it was easier said than done.

Passing down the business wasn't just about me and my family. It concerned my clients and employees. They were like family, so I couldn't simply sell and walk away. My business was built around relationships. We grew together over many years. How could I satisfy myself, my family, and my clients?

We had to figure out how the business was going to transition. We had to decide who was capable of being an owner to keep this business going beyond me. Could one of my sons do it? I have two sons who couldn't be more different from each other. One works in the business; the other lives across the country and is in the Canadian Navy. I couldn't imagine them working together. What about a spouse? A key employee? Oh boy, I needed to figure this out.

My life was simple, but what if there had been a second marriage? What if there were children from that marriage or stepchildren? All of a sudden, it could become complicated and overwhelming.

I had to figure out how to give one of my boys a share of the business yet make things equitable for the other. Or did I? I had to figure it out on my own, how to do everything. There were so many things I wish I had known. I wish I had started my planning earlier. I wish I had had a better system. I wish I had known who I could ask for help.

This book is my answer to those wishes, for you. Do the things I describe in this book now, so you don't have to call for help later.

According to Stats Canada, as of December 2020 there are 1.22 million employer businesses in Canada[1]. Of those, 97.9 percent (1.2 million) have fewer than one hundred employees.

Of those, 63 percent are family owned. Yet fewer than 34 percent of family small businesses have a documented, understood succession plan. Some may think they have a plan, but either it's not documented or it's not understood by everyone involved. I wish there were statistics for "Have you even discussed it?" I can't imagine how low that number would be.

Most first-generation family business owners are so busy running the business, and they face so many complexities and challenges when they think about succession planning, that they only start to deal with it when there is a conflict or a crisis. That's when I get called. But it's possible to deal with and prevent some of these conflicts and crises before they arise. Why not start now? It is never too early or too late—as Nike says, "Just do it."

Most of the family business clients we work with at my firm, BlueRoots, have modest savings and retirement accounts. Maybe that sounds like you. If you built the business from the ground up, it's likely that most of your wealth is in the business.

When you made money over the years, you invested it back into the business. Perhaps you started as a plumber. You worked for

---

[1] Government of Canada, Innovation, Science and Economic Development Canada, Office of the Deputy Minister, Small Business, Tourism and Marketplace Services. 2021. "Key Small Business Statistics — 2021." December 22, 2021. https://ised-isde.canada.ca/site/sme-research-statistics/en/key-small-business-statistics/key-small-business-statistics-2021.

somebody before you set out on your own. You put all your money into trucks and equipment as you grew, and you hired people to help you as the business grew with your reputation. You did that for maybe twenty-five to thirty years, and over the last five or ten, as your reputation has grown, the money has really started coming in. You're seeing a return on all that hard work and investment, and now you want to step back and enjoy it. But how? Have you even discussed it? Are your kids ready to take it over? Are they even interested? Are they capable? Are you ready to let go? Maybe you should just sell to one of your competitors—that would solve many problems.

Let's say your kids want to get involved. Have you had a discussion around how to come into the business? Are they looking to buy in? Can they afford to buy it outright? Could they buy in at a level they can afford? Can you depend on them to run the business well, so it can afford to pay you regular dividends and pay them a salary? Can you even make that happen? Is it possible? Some days probably not. So many unanswered questions.

But it is possible. This book is not for people who intend to sell to a third party. If you are a first-generation founder and thinking about passing on your success while keeping the business in the family, this book is for you. If you are a second-generation family member starting to think about what will happen when your parents are no longer involved in the business, or how to get more involved, then this book is also for you. If you're still not sure on what to do with your business when you exit, this book can help you as well.

What You'll Find in This Book

We work with small, family-owned, first- and second-generation businesses. In every family, we see dynamics play out in three areas: the Business, the Owners, and the Family. These areas overlap, but they are not the same. Everything is tied together, but it can be teased apart. That "teasing apart" is an important part of what we do, and we've used our approach to structure this book. You will see chapters on Business, Owners, and Family, and yes, they overlap, but they are distinctive. We cover a lot of topics in this book, but they are all rooted in the same concept: preparing a family business for succession.

"Succession" can mean many things. It could mean passing the business on to family members or selling it to a competitor, or to employees, or to a private equity firm. It could mean shutting it down. It could mean continuing to work in it even as other family members take on more responsibilities. The definition of a happy succession event is unique to each family. But the bones of a good succession are always the same.

- Ensuring all the relevant family members are appropriately involved in decision-making and communicate well with each other.

- Creating a vision for the future and seeing it through.

- Understanding the three perspectives unique to family business—Family, Owner, and Business—and how they influence decisions, plans, and actions.

- Getting the right help at the right time to make the right decisions.

Often, I meet founders who are their own worst enemy. They say they want to get out of the business, but they cannot bring themselves to relinquish control. They stand in the way of the very growth that is necessary for the business to survive because they don't trust the next generation, who likely wants to do things differently than they did. They are afraid of change, which often comes down to questions of trust. They may be looking at their children the way parents tend to, seeing them as kids who couldn't even remember to take out the garbage, and conclude there is no way they can hand the business to them.

This is not unique to you, nor is it a recipe for a smooth succession. But it can be addressed.

We are not here to tell you what to do. True, we tell our clients what to do every day. That's because we know our clients and their unique situations and can come up with the right solution for each of them. Even though small businesses are similar, they are not all the same.

Rather than tell you what to do, I wrote this book to help you think—to think about your situation from a fresh perspective, to think about your problems with new insights, to think about your options with a new understanding of what is possible. As you go through the book, you'll find prompts to help guide you toward the most appropriate information.

You're reading this book because, even if it's just in the back of your mind, something is bothering you. You need help finding answers. If we were working face-to-face with you, the first thing we do is understand the nature of the challenges you face, so we can tailor our advice. Since we can't have a conversation through the pages of this book, we're asking you to have that conversation with yourself by using our prompts and questionnaires.

This book doesn't have exact answers for you; we want you to use it as a road map. Many business owners, when they think about planning for the future, will consult with a lawyer or an accountant who works with them. While that can be useful, remember that those individuals have a particular perspective on a particular slice of your business and your life. We believe in a collaborative approach, bringing all advisors together, allowing our family business practice to take a holistic look at the owners, the family, and the business. Because of that, in these pages we are able to give you a fuller picture of what you may want to think about and the questions you may want to ask.

If you are like many of the family businesses we work with, you don't even know what you don't know! At a minimum, we intend to address that. Even if you finish this book without firm answers, you can be confident that you are seeing the entire playing field and know where to focus.

As the owner and face of the business, your skill and reputation have made you successful—perhaps more successful than you thought you would be when you started out. Now, your business has grown beyond what you know and what you've learned at school and on the job.

Maybe you don't even know why you are in the business beyond paying the bills. Maybe you feel you are out of your league. What's the larger goal? What are you trying to do? Grow and run an empire? Grow it and sell it? Support a nice lifestyle? Have you ever really thought about the reason you do what you do?

It is time to refocus and work on the business, not in the business. You might be tired of that line, but it is true. Working on the business is about strategy, vision, succession. You get so busy that it gets pushed down the list. Now is the time to bring it to the top. You spend most of your time working in the business. You're getting tired of the day-to-day grind. Working 24-7 is not as appealing or as necessary as it once was.

You will notice a theme in my approach: pretty much every solution I discuss in this book—solutions to the problems you face—will involve some kind of growth. Growth gives you the resources to do what you want to do, such as hand the business to a new generation, sell it for top dollar, or retire and live off the dividends while someone else operates it.

A lot of business owners don't realize that if they want to save for retirement, they need to count on more than just the business as a retirement income source. They need to diversify, depending on what the best solution is for them. It could be in a Registered Retirement Savings Plan (RRSP), Individual Pension Plan (IPP), Tax-Free Savings Account (TFSA), or some other means of saving outside of the company.

Even if business owners do plan to sell their company and live off the proceeds, many don't operate in a way that's going to get them the most value when that time comes. Often, the result is that the owner hits retirement age and realizes that they have to keep working to continue to generate revenue for the company, so they have something to live on. They can't afford to retire, and their business can't afford to lose them.

We find this problem is most common among small business owners. They're so used to working and keeping their head down, focused on working in the business, that it doesn't occur to them to prepare for the future—until one day they lift their head up and realize they're older and can't continue to work at this pace. They are too busy working *in* the business rather than *on* the business.

Sometimes we see businesses where the owner is the business—there really isn't much else. This can be the case in a service business such as consulting. If there are no assets, there are no sources of renewing revenue. If there is no value from recurring revenue, it's hard to sell the business. That doesn't mean such an owner can't retire; it just means they must plan differently.

Typically, you need two people to replace a retiring owner because that owner wore a lot of different hats, they worked 24-7, and they have a lot of knowledge in all aspects of the business. That's expensive to replace at a moment's notice. Doing it right means you need time and growth, which means you need a plan to make that happen. That's all part of succession planning.

This book introduces you to the kinds of conversations you must have—potentially difficult conversations at first—and who to have them with. It gives guidance on what kinds of questions to ask yourself and others, and what areas of your business, family, and yourself you should focus on as you prepare your business for whatever is coming next.

It is essential that you do the things outlined in this book when you are thinking about handing the reins to the next generation, slowing down, or selling your business. It's also incredibly useful to do them even if you are going to carry on working for years. The sooner you start thinking and planning, the easier it will be. Don't get me wrong, it can still be done quickly, but it is more stressful and harder on the business and family. The principles underlying everything we teach are helpful to all family businesses at all stages. What we want is for your business to work for you—rather than you work for your business. We want to help you achieve the vision you desire, and not be a slave to a creation you can't manage as well as you'd like. What makes a business ready to sell or pass down also simply makes a business better. Better for you, better for your family, better for your employees, better for your clients and customers.

Beginning with my experience in my own company, extending to our many clients, I have lost track of how often I have said or heard the phrase, "If only I had known that twenty (or ten or five) years ago." I have said that to myself many times over the last thirty-plus years. After many years of being frustrated and banging my head against a wall, I learned there are answers and help available if you know how and where to look for them.

This is the "what I wish I had known" book that gives you the benefit of the collective experience of scores of business owners like you.

Why Listen to Me?

Well, probably much like you, I started in my industry (financial services) in my twenties, I was young, I needed money, my friends and family said, "You can sell anything, you should get into a sales career." (This was after the advertising agency I was working for went bankrupt and my paycheck bounced.) I was desperate for money to pay my rent and eat. I quickly learned that I was good at selling. However, I was selling a product that was not based on a *need*.

Need selling was something I was passionate about; I wouldn't sell you something I wouldn't buy myself. So, I left my employer and went out on my own, I made the switch to need selling, and I expanded my knowledge and skill set as my clientele grew and changed.

I got my CLU (extensive knowledge in the insurance industry) to help my clients put the right coverage in place to protect their family and business. As my clients aged with me, needs became more complex, so along came the CFP (expertise in the areas of financial planning, tax, estate planning, and retirement).

Every new stage of my business was a huge learning curve, and I had to do the learning and research on my own. No one I knew was selling on the needs of the entire family and their business.

Over the years I became more passionate about helping others like me—first-generation, family-run businesses. That lead me to the FEA designation (Family Enterprise Advisor). And finally, as my clients, like myself, amassed wealth inside and outside the business, I got my TEP (specialists in inheritance and succession planning, wills, and trusts). If I had had a mentor to help me with the growing pains of owning a first-generation business, I would have saved myself a great deal of stress.

Alas, here I am now, with a wealth of knowledge and experience, ready to help guide you through your succession journey.

It may seem daunting to prepare your family business for the handoff of your success, but remember what they say: "How do you eat an elephant? One bite at a time." You can think big but take one bite at a time.

SUCCESS QUESTIONS

Since we can't have a conversation with you in the pages of this book, our success questions are meant to get you thinking. You will be able to narrow down what your focus should be with these questions.

Grab a sheet of paper now. Being open and honest with yourself will be the hardest part.

Don't skip over this exercise!

Not every question will be relevant to you—that's OK. Focus on the ones that matter. This will help you to break down your business and understand where you need help most.

As you read each one, think of someone asking you the question. What is the first answer that comes to mind? Write it down.

- What do you hope to get out of this book?

- What is your ideal outcome for passing on your success?

- How long is your runway for making a transition?

- Have you already started your transition?

- Do you want to keep your business in the family?

CHAPTER 1

WHAT DO YOU WANT AND HOW ARE YOU GETTING THERE?

"A painting is never finished—it simply stops in interesting places."
—DAN SULLIVAN, Author of *Who Not How: The Formula to Achieve Bigger Goals Through Accelerating Teamwork*

Succession or transition, whatever you want to call it, is one of those aspects of family-run business that's easier said than done. It sounds simple, but typically the first-generation doesn't have the knowledge or time to implement the transition—you're too busy building up and running the business. You poured your blood and sweat into it, and you didn't have a nickel to your name in the first ten years. You just got grief for not being home. Or in my case, you're made to feel horrible by your kids. My son once asked me, "Mama, why are you always at work?" I said, "To make money." He came home later that week with money he had made at school. I still have that in my office as a reminder of the importance of balance.

As someone who works daily in your business, you're good at what you do. Maybe you (or your dad, or your granddad) started off working for someone else, but at some point, you realized you could make more money on your own. You could have more freedom. You could run your own life. Be your own boss. That was all very appealing.

So, you started out on your own, swinging a hammer, wrenching pipes, twisting wires, selling your services. You did well. There was demand. You got some more trucks. You expanded your services. You gained confidence, got ambitious, taking on bigger and better jobs.

Your skill at your craft brought you success. Success brought new challenges. When you needed help with the books, your spouse, other relative, or friend stepped in to keep the money in the family. After all, it's hard to justify hiring someone, and a good-quality person costs a lot of money.

Kids came along, and you were starting to make some money, so you set aside an account for college or university. Maybe one of the kids went to business school or learned a trade. You needed help, and that's what they're doing now—helping you. But they don't know how to do what you do. They didn't come up in the business like you did. They have different skills, and you're not sure how they will fit in the business long term.

If you're one of the second-generation family members working in the business, you have ideas, a vision. You want to do stuff, but Dad and Mom want to keep doing things their way, and your siblings either have other ideas or don't want to be involved at all. Sure, the first generation has experience. But you have education. You know things they don't. And you want a chance to show them what you can do. How do you get everyone on board?

Getting Everyone on the Same Page

The first generation in a family business figures out how they like to do things, what works for them and the clients they serve. They have honed their skill by trial and error. They have been doing it for many years and have generally not had a mentor to guide them. They have learned and adapted along the way.

Typically, when the second generation comes in, they have new ideas, lots of education and information at their fingertips. The second gens find themselves trying to get the first generation on board, but they're often met with resistance along the lines of, "We do it this way because we've always done it this way." Those differing approaches can become a real issue in the organization, especially if the second generation is taking on more authority in the business or bringing in or managing employees. It is complicated by the fact they are related. Family dinners still need to happen, and tension will carry over from work. How you deal with an employee who is family is much different than a nonfamily employee.

This can become a real pain point, and like so many, it's rooted in assumptions and in communication. We like to say, "When you think about vision, don't think about the mom's vision, or the son's vison—think about the entire vision. What is the vision of everyone together?" They must get on the same page. That doesn't mean giving in; it means allowing everyone to be heard and doing what is best for the company and the family. Open and honest conversations will lead to everyone being on the same page. It is not easy, but it needs to be done.

Someone must take the lead in this communication. That's how you are going to build the transition from one generation to the next. It's going to take some time—but if you don't put in the time, it isn't going to happen. For example, key employees may decide they would rather work somewhere else because there is too much drama, they don't know what is happening, it threatens their livelihood and future plans. The business can really suffer, and the transition planning or whatever comes next can be jeopardized.

Why Family Businesses Fail and How to Beat the Odds

According to the *Harvard Business Review*, 70 percent of family businesses don't make it to the second generation[2].

That means nearly three quarters of small business owners never get to pass their success down to their children. They either sell it, or they shut down. Only 13 percent make it to the third generation and 3 percent make it to the fourth and beyond, according to John Ward.

We think that's a shame. When an owner builds a business from the ground up, that business is their baby. Those owners are the backbone of the company and part of a community. When they shut down or merge into a larger company, the "family" aspect is lost. Frankly, that

2   https://hbr.org/2012/01/avoid-the-traps-that-can-destroy-family-businesses

makes us sad. We like family businesses, I am a family business, and our mission is to "successfully navigate the unique reality of working with family in business," in part to help the families who start and run their business get what they want from it.

It has taken me many years of struggle and lots of education to truly understand what I was going through and how much harder it is when family is involved.

According to *The Globe and Mail,* the top ten reasons family businesses fail are as follows:

- Poor succession planning

- Lack of trusted advisors

- Family conflict

- Different visions between generations

- Governance challenges

- Exclusion of family members outside the business

- Unprepared next-generation leaders

- Poor strategic planning

- Unclear plan for future growth

- Lack of financial planning

Regardless of the report you read, when you're moving from first generation to second or from second to third, communication between family, business, and ownership is the most important element in allowing a family business to survive and thrive. With open lines of communication, you build trust. We will touch more on the importance of communication in the next chapter.

This book's focus is on how to beat the odds and how to structure a successful transition of a family business.

We don't believe that 70 percent of owners *prefer* not to hand the business over to their children. Something else is at work. In our experience, the top challenges to creating a smooth and successful succession are these:

- Owners' hesitation to pass on to a specific family member because of concerns about education, communication, expectations, merit, or entitlement.

- Thinking about your own mortality.

- Comparing yourself with the next generation.

- Lack of strategy to transition.

- Being unwilling or not knowing how to let go.

I want you to know that family businesses also have many advantages:

- Family control: decisions are made quickly, leaders are nimble, and they can respond and change direction swiftly in any situation.

- Emotional attachment to employees and clients: they are like family, and leaders want the best for them.

- Social ties to the community: leaders have connections at both a family and business level, in both social events and philanthropy.

- Continuity: there is a longer time horizon, there are no shareholders to answer to, it's not always about the money, and social and environmental issues can take the lead.

- Great relationships with suppliers: long-term relationships turn into a two-way street; suppliers can be counted on in a pinch and vice versa.

Remember that family businesses are a major player in the overall economy, but more importantly they are essential pillars in your community. It is important to look at the positives of keeping it a family business and passing on your success.

Talking about Today and Tomorrow

A lot of what I write about in this book has to do with succession or transition—whether to pass a business along, how to do that, or how to sell it. But the problems we discuss in the coming pages are not *only* about succession. They are problems that can and do afflict any growing and successful family business at almost any time.

In my experience, most founders of family businesses have been too focused on making the business a success to pick their head up and look down the road at the future. Most of the time, they don't have family meetings to talk about the business; most family members are kept in the dark. Usually, some sort of event such as a health scare forces questions about the future to the surface.

If family members begin talking to each other, they may realize they have wildly different assumptions about everything from what the business does, to who can be involved, to what it is worth, to who would inherit it, to whether it could be sold, to what is fair for everyone involved.

Even if you plan to keep working in your own company for decades, you may encounter and need to address the kinds of problems we see every day—problems around hiring and retention, around operations and compliance, around growth and guidance. How you handle these problems absolutely matters to the success of your business not only in the future—whatever your vision for the future is—but also today.

In small family businesses the lines get blurred between family and business planning. The business is the tail that wags the family dog. This should be reversed. Family and business need to be looked at independently but together. Each element is looked at from a different perspective.

Where Are You Going?

Before you figure out how to get somewhere, you must know where you are going. The same thing is true in your family business. You must understand where you are, and where you are trying to go before you come up with a plan for how to get there. There is a big difference between a plan and an idea. A plan is actionable; an idea is just that—an idea, no action attached. Change that by building a plan with all your ideas. This can happen over many family meetings. Business becomes easier if you have a plan that you can follow and measure, or at least see where you went off course if it is not going the way you anticipated.

Maybe you have a clear succession plan. Or maybe you really don't know what you want to do. That's OK. You'd be amazed at how many family business owners like you have barely even thought about the future or the kinds of questions I ask. Lots of business owners I meet have been so busy that they haven't created the time and mental space to answer some fundamental questions for themselves.

When we start working with family clients, our first question is, "Why are we here?" In the rest of this chapter, we're going to help you answer that question without us sitting in the room with you: Why are we—you and us—here?

For instance, if you want to keep the company in the family but don't want an active role anymore, the way forward involves having important discussions about succession with your family and determining what type of ownership will make everyone happy going forward.

Or, if there is something about your career that you really love, but the business is exhausting you, then the way forward involves figuring out how to change your business so you can get back to spending most of your time on what you love.

Or, if you feel ready to move on completely—and your kids have no interest in succession whatsoever—then the way forward involves trying to get the most value out of selling your business.

Those are three very different outcomes, but achieving any of them requires you to move your business toward being a self-reliant operation. By "self-reliant," I mean a business that doesn't need you to be involved in the day-to-day operations to thrive. Only then will you be able to do what you want and get the most value in the process—not only financial value but family value and personal value.

In almost every instance, when we work with clients, we help them move toward some expression of a self-reliant company: a company that you run, rather than a company that runs you.

Many business owners think there is no alternative to a life that has been taken over by their company. They don't know how to stop doing what they have been doing for the last thirty years. It has been all-consuming. Starting a business is hard work. It takes a lot of time, determination, stick-to-itiveness, and compromise. This is not a pain point; it's just the way things are. It can feel like you have no choice; this is just what you have always done and continue to do to keep things running. But that's not true!

Life is much better if you are doing more of what you love to do. That seems simple enough, but you'd be surprised by how few people take the time to think this through. When you do, you may find that you can really love your work, if you can stick to the parts that you love and find other people to do the parts you don't. The hardest part is letting go.

Everything in this book is oriented around that idea. No matter what outcome you want, if you're reading this book, you want something different than what you have now, or you need a game plan to get what you want. Some version of a self-reliant company will get you closer to your goal. You'll see us come back to that idea again and again.

SUCCESS QUESTIONS

We've provided the following success questions below for you to start thinking. Not every question will be relevant to you—that's OK. Focus on the ones that matter. This will help you to break down your business and understand where you need help most.

As you read each one, think of someone asking you the question, what is the first answer that comes to mind? Write it down.

- What makes you truly happy? (This doesn't have to be work related, but it could be, i.e., fishing, knitting, meeting with clients, seeing a project completed—what makes you smile?)

- Make a list of everything you do in a typical day. Leave no task out; nothing is too small: making coffee, answering the phone, quoting, talking to clients, visiting job sites, research. Once the list is complete, go through each item and ask yourself, "Do I enjoy this? Does this make me happy?" Answer yes or no next to it. Even if you are good at it, if you don't enjoy it or it doesn't make you happy, mark it no.

- What needs to happen for you to get to that ideal day of, *I enjoy this, it makes me happy to come into work*? (Can you delegate, outsource, or hire someone for the role? Or do you need to grow the company to have your ideal day? What can you do, what can you control?)

- What future role, if any, do you want? Mentoring, sales, troubleshooting, retirement?

- Have you discussed succession or transition planning with your family? Does your family know what you really want?

- Are you postponing things until you "retire" (i.e., are you postponing the boat purchase until you retire and have time to enjoy it)?

- Are you working for financial reasons? Do you need the income the business provides to live on?

- Do you wake up excited to go to work?

- If you have multiple businesses, is one your favourite?
  - Why is it your favourite?

- What keeps you up at night?

CHAPTER 2

THE IMPORTANCE OF FAMILY AND BUSINESS COMMUNICATION

"Communication—the human connection—is the key to personal and career success."
—PAUL J. MEYER, Co-Founder and President of The Commons Project

How many times have you said or heard, "You never tell me anything! I have to drag it out of you." Communication or the lack of it has been the demise of many relationships, personal and business. Communication is everywhere: at work, with your pets, with family and friends. You can't get away from it. It is the key to success in all relationships, and almost everything else in life. Since we are constantly communicating, why is it so hard to do it effectively? Why is it so hard to communicate with the people we are closest to, our family?

- I asked some of my family members, "Why are you not in the family business?" I received a variety of answers:

- I was never asked.

- Didn't know it was an option.

- It was a male/female dominated business, only the boys/girls went to work in the company.

- I am not interested in sales, trades, trucking, etc.

- I want to have my own business.

- I couldn't work with my family.

I have heard them all. The main reason for family members not participating in the business, in my opinion, is lack of communication within the family. Avoidance of a difficult or sensitive conversation is the most common reason for lack of partnership that I have seen. If you want to pass on your success and keep it a family business, communication will be your best friend. Don't be scared of it.

Not only do you need to understand all the elements of communicating, but you must have effective and frequent family communication. It is very important to understand each of your family members' styles. They are not all the same; they are all very different, just like you. Taking the time to understand each other a bit better, understanding why they do the things they do and how they like to be communicated with, will make for a stronger family, which will lead to a stronger business.

It took me a long time to figure this out. But when I took the time to really understand my husband and boys and their differences, communication and tolerance levels went way up. And my stress level went down. Another one of those *I wish I had done it earlier* moments. But we get so wrapped up in growing the business we don't take the time to truly see our family has changed and grown up, and that our communication style is no longer *my way or the highway*. Our families want to be treated and should be treated like the adults they are or are becoming. Interestingly, overcommunicating has never been an issue a family has brought up to me. But body language, tone, or lack of communication has for sure.

If one of the biggest family breakdowns is due in part to the lack of communication or a misunderstanding, how do you even start to fix that? Start with the knowledge that effective communication has three elements:

- Body language: the visible actions that we show to others using all parts of our body (55 percent)

- Voice: the pitch, pace, tone, and volume of our voice (38 percent)

- Words: the actual words that make up our message (7 percent)

You have probably heard this mentioned in the past—that even when we don't think we are communicating, we are, mainly using our body language. Voice and words are an important element for sure, but body language accounts for over half of our communication. It is the unspoken part of communication, the actions that we show to others, that has the biggest impact on getting our message across. Sometimes the wrong message.

I can remember coming out of a meeting with my son, who had just started working with me in the business at twenty-four years old. I asked him what was wrong. He said nothing was wrong. I asked him why he sat there the whole time leaning back in his chair with his arms crossed and not saying a word. He said he was just taking it all in. To me it looked like he was disengaged. How could I consider having him take on a bigger role or even consider at some point to pass down my success to him when he looked like he didn't want to be there?

Even without words, miscommunication happens all the time. Think of when you are talking to someone and they are slouched, have their arms crossed, or when your child or parent rolls their eyes at you. They haven't said anything, but you are already forming an opinion or getting mad, and the situation goes downhill fast.

Using your voice's pitch, pace, tone, and volume accounts for 38 percent of communication. Remember when your kids would say "wwwhhhyyy" in a high-pitched voice? It was like nails on a chalkboard.

The tone of that one word could send you over the edge.

It is hard to believe, but the words we use account for only 7 percent of the overall message we are trying to convey. A very important element, but surprising that it is such a small part of the overall form of communication. I probably would have reversed them if I had to guess the answer while playing a trivia game.

As I have mentioned, communication is the biggest issue to tackle in a family business. Communication is not just talking to someone. It includes the frequency, the message itself, and all three of the elements mentioned previously. To be able to pass on your success, you must use all the tools available to you to develop your plan and see your vision come to fruition.

Depending on your personal preference, you will use a different percentage of each communication tool—face-to-face, video call, phone, and email—but they will *all* still come into play. They all must align to get the message you want to get across, in a way to engage the person you are talking to.

One-word answers on an email might seem curt and seem like you are upset or don't care. When, in fact, you were busy and just wanted to respond before you forgot. Too many exclamation points may also be construed the wrong way. NO!!!!!!! I think that is the email form of yelling with a high-pitched tone …hard-stop no.

People always used to think I was upset about something when I wrote a quick response in email. I wasn't. I just answered the question in a direct way with only a couple of words. Now, however, I'm very aware of how people can interpret this sort of response, so I'm much better at knowing how to be congenial in my emails. Even in an email your tone can shine through. Be very careful with the structure and the words you use. "No!" versus "Not at this time."

It is important to remember that the form of communication we use is our own preference and not necessarily that of the others around us. This applies to communicating within your family and your business. I like bullet points and short answers on emails or reports.

If I need more information, I will ask for it or do the research myself. Those who know me know that many times I will respond with a very short answer—not, *hi, how ya doing?* It is just the answer—*yep*, *nope*, *do it*. I am not being curt, nor am I upset; I am just answering the question. If you want more details, you can ask for it up front or come back and ask for it. Others, and we all know them, will send a two-page email when two lines would have done the trick in our minds.

We are all different and we need to understand each other to make communication more effective. Both at home and at work. Have some tolerance; just like everyone is not going to send you bullet points, you are not going to send two-page emails. That is just who you are. Learn to adapt and appreciate them for who they are.

The Three Parts of the Human Mind

Not only is it crucial to understand the three parts of communication, but it's also critical to know about the three parts of the mind: the thinking IQ (cognitive), the feeling EQ (affective), and the doing AQ (action quotient, conative).

The thinking part or IQ deals with the skills, reason, knowledge, experience, and education of a person. The feeling or EQ is a person's motivation, attitudes, preferences, emotions, and values—more their personality traits. Doing or AQ deals with a person's actions, their drive, their instinct, necessity, mental energy, innate force, and talents. Once you realize different parts of the brain deal with different areas it is easier to start the process of understanding and building effective communication strategies.

The easiest part to understand is cognitive/thinking/IQ. Skill set, education, and knowledge are easily figured out. Are you an electrician, yes or no? Pretty easy to get the answers to the IQ portion.

Feeling and doing are a little harder to put your finger on. Not only your own tendencies, but your family members' as well. Why is understanding how a person thinks and how a person does things important in communication? An element of effective communication is understanding both the reason people do what they do (how they be-have) and the natural instincts of those people (how they do things). You should also understand yourself.

By having a better understanding of each other you will have more tolerance and patience, and you will understand where your differences can be leveraged to become stronger together. The goal is to pass on your success. The best way to do that is by communicating your vison and plans.

Let's dig into EQ/AQ a bit. I am not an expert, but Dr. Paul Hertz, the founder and architect of the revolutionary PRINT® system of im-proving personal, interpersonal, and organizational outcomes, is. He has been studying behaviours for over thirty years. He has uncovered the *why* of behaviours, not just the *what*. He has developed nine un-conscious motivators® that we all fall into. We have major and minor motivators, and that combination is what makes us unique.

It is not a personality test; it is a motivational model. Why is this important? If you understand why people do what they do, you can have better lines of communication and build stronger relationships. Those relationships can be in your family or your business. We tend to want to surround ourselves with people like us, who have the same beliefs and education levels, and we tend to attack each problem the same way. However, unlike choosing our friends, we cannot choose our family members, which can result in tension, conflicts. Once you learn and understand that we all have different unconscious motiva-tors®, why people do what they do, you realize that we are all required to make the world go round. That pushback or conflict you may be experiencing is just because of the way they process information and how they act on it.

Another expert is Kathy Kolbe. Kathy is the founder of Kolbe Corp and the Center for Conative Abilities. She was driven to more fully understand what drives human performance and began her own re-search and development of the first conative assessment. According to Kolbe.com, the organization has been working to bring insight and understanding that helps people and organizations achieve their goals for more than forty years.[3]

The result of her many years of research led her to develop the Kolbe A™ Index. Kolbe assessments help you understand how you naturally approach tasks and work. The assessment describes how you start every project and when you are free to be yourself. An example might be this: you are having a family party, so do you start by thinking about what you did in the past or do you have a million new ideas as soon as someone mentions party?

I did both the PRINT® and Kolbe assessments at work and at home, and what a difference it made. We used them at the office, but I decided to try it at home as well. I knew how it helped at work, so I was sure it could help at home as well. It certainly couldn't hurt.

The communication between me and my youngest was a struggle. Just understanding that we are all different and approach things from different angles can be an eye-opener. How many times have you said, "That can't be my kid. I would have done that first thing, not waited until the last minute. That must come from the other side of the family." Nope, we are all different and we need to embrace those differences.

With the success of using Kolbe and PRINT® at work and at home, I became certified in both so I could help other families and their businesses become stronger.

One of the things I learned at home was how to work together and have open and honest conversations. Understanding and sharing how I like to be approached and communicated with was a game changer. I am a quick-to-make-decisions kind of person; good or bad, right or wrong, I make it and move on. My husband and sons like to think more about a situation before making a decision. Although I may want an answer immediately, I cannot spring anything new on them and expect to get my result on the spot. That gets very frustrating for me. However, I have learned to give and take, and so have they.

---

3   "The History of Kolbe Corp." n.d. https://www.kolbe.com/our-history/

None of us are going to change, so let's save ourselves conflict by starting the conversation with something like this: "I know you need time to think about this, but I need/would like an answer by the end of the day/in an hour on this issue." Don't do it every time, but on occasion you can ask for a quick turnaround. It saves conflict and pushback, which can lead to a bit of a spat.

If you don't learn to talk it out or set the parameters, a conversation can drop down into "you always" statements and then, as mentioned earlier, go downhill real fast. Remember the time five years ago when you did something once and it has now turned into all the time? Yep, been there.

Understanding the three elements of communication, the three parts of the brain, and the modes of preferred communication were instrumental in my success journey. Sometimes you must be at the end of your rope to make a change. We tend to think the next generation should be just like us to carry on our success. Or if you are the next generation, you may tend to think you are not your parents so you can't possibly take over the business. That is not true at all. By having open, honest, and frequent communication, you can achieve your vision, build a plan, and gain the courage with the support of your family to move forward.

Whatever it takes, move the awareness of communication to the forefront of your mind. It will help in all areas of family, friends, and business relationships.

Again, communication is much more than just the words we speak. It is about written words as well. We all have a different form of written communication style.

Many people like paper lists, while others prefer to have the to-do list emailed to them. I like something written down; I still carry a notepad to write things down. I think that is a generational thing. My son prefers an email or taking notes on his computer. We have compromised at work. I am getting better at using the computer for notes and lists (I still use a pen and paper at home), but it is a struggle for me. I have learned to embrace his knowledge and comfort level of technology. I have let him take the lead on updating the processes and choosing programs to make us more efficient and have better communication within the whole company. Technology is not going away anytime soon. We can't have two different processes in place.

Although we are talking about family communication, this does apply to the office. My assistant of many years and I have learned how to work together even with our completely different styles of how we communicate and how we approach things to get them done. Our communication has developed by being open and honest with each other and having difficult conversations. She understands what I do and don't do well, and we have agreed to compromise on how we get things accomplished. We need each other's strengths to be productive and grow the company.

At the beginning, the hardest part for her was to be open and honest with me. To have the hard conversations with me on how we can work together more efficiently, and what part I needed to play to make it happen. Even though I am her boss, in order for her to do her job and keep us following my vision and the plan we put in place, she has to bring me back in line, stop my giving her drive-by requests or procrastinating on getting notes to her to get into the files. She can't do the job she was hired for if I am not doing my part.

We all get off course sometimes. Why is it so hard at home to have those conversations when we fall out of sync? Why don't we compromise at home, help each other get back on track? If we don't work effectively together at home, we will be in conflict all the time, and that is not fun for anyone. And succession is off the table because it is never discussed.

Understand Your Kids for the Adults They've Become

At what point do we stop treating our kids like kids and treat them like the adults they are or are becoming? When do we start to talk to them like adults? I think that is the hardest part of a family and family business and why the struggle to bring our next generations into the business is hard. We continually see them as our kids. I would constantly go back to the actions of my kids during their childhood and base everything on that. I would communicate as mother to son, instead of adult to adult. It took me a long time to let that go and appreciate my sons' knowledge today and their current contributions to society.

We need to listen to and appreciate our kids and their ideas, have them work with us, not for us. Remember how much smarter we were than our parents? How we had to set the flashing twelve on the VCR for them? Now I need my kids set up the Google home system and update it as necessary. Embrace their generation's knowledge and have open and honest conversations with them. Make sure you are all on the same page. Remember they can make major contributions if you let them. Edmond H. Fischer said, "It is commonly said that a teacher fails if he has not been surpassed by his students." Let's hope they surpass us. Pass on your success and let them run with it!

Now that you understand the importance of good communication, it's time to put everything together and explore a critical model that explains the three circles of family businesses.[4]

The Family Business Model
Understanding the three-circle model and visualizing it was my biggest breakthrough. Once I really looked at it, it all made sense. The three-circle model is the foundation to understanding a family business. It has been around helping family businesses since it was developed in the 1970s by Harvard Business School professors Renato Tagiuri and John A. Davis. It was this nugget of information that changed how I thought about and planned for the future success of my family business. I began to truly understand and appreciate my role in the business and the role of my family members.

---

4   https://johndavis.com/three-circle-model-family-business-system/

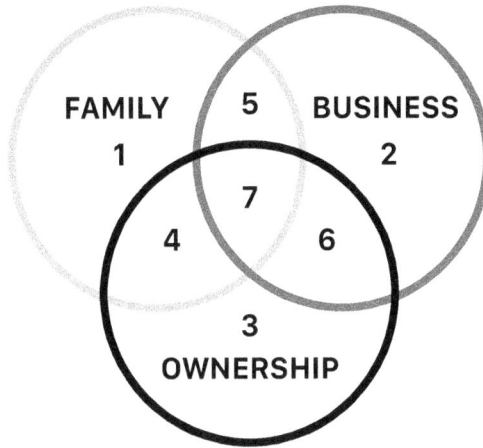

1 - Family only
2 - Business only
3 - Ownership only
4 - Family with Ownership

5 - Family in the Business
6 - Business with Ownership
7 - Family in the Business
   with Ownership

Within the three-circle model are seven different points of view. Some overlap and some do not. Each position has a unique perspective. Understanding where you, your family members, and your employees sit will help you understand what lens they are looking through when they ask a question. What is their perspective compared to yours?

Since each circle has its own perspective, depending on where people sit, they will look at or be concerned only with issues from their point of view. Issues in the other seats are not on their radar at all.

The founder or owner of the business will at some point generally sit in number seven, the intersection of the three circles in this diagram, meaning they are in all three circles at the same time; they work in the business, they own the business, and they are part of the family. At different moments they will adopt different perspectives, but they always hold all three points of view. When they wear the business hat, they are generally thinking, *What does this mean from the perspective of the business?* When they wear the ownership hat, *What does this mean for me, the owner?* When they wear the family hat, *What does this mean for my family?* In my experience, most of the time you don't think of where your decisions are coming from. You are just making decisions, like I was.

My COO Lori would say to me long before I understood the three-circle model, "Where is that idea coming from?" She would say, "Are you saying that as an owner of the business or an employee of the business?" That made sense to me. I would answer with whichever approach I was taking, business or ownership. Then it would make more sense to me and to her. Over the years we shortened it to, *Hat? Business.* No need for more explanation.

The lines between the hats are blurry most of the time when you are a first-generation owner, so it's important to ask yourself frequently what hat you are wearing when you answer a question or come up with an idea. You likely wear all of them daily. You're the one who chats with the clients. You're the one who does the quotes. You're the one who lies awake at night thinking about problems. You're the one who may bring in the majority of the family income. It's important to ask yourself, as you grapple with problems, what issue am I dealing with? Is this a business problem, a family problem, an ownership problem?

Other people around you are likely to hold just one or two points of view. Family members may look only at the income side of the business. They want to make sure the money is coming in to pay for school, cars, and vacations. They don't know or care much about what the business does on a day-to-day basis. But they might wonder about how any changes in the business will impact their family life, or what certain decisions mean for different family members. The people who work in the business as employees will think about work-related issues, like work–life balance or benefits and wages.

It is very important to be mindful that, when a family member questions something you have said or done, they do not have the full picture. They see a glimpse of the entire entity. They are coming at it with only one or two hats, depending on where they sit in the three-circle model.

As you start to think about the questions and decisions your business faces, be mindful of which hat you're wearing. This may be a challenge at the beginning; I know it was for me. Most owners wear all three most of the time and aren't disciplined to understand which perspective is winning out when they make a decision. Until you understand what each of those three circles in the Venn diagram means and their points of view, you won't make wise, self-aware decisions.

This framework gives you a set of lenses or hats with which to understand the problems you're wrestling with. When you understand that these perspectives exist, you'll be able to better appreciate where someone is coming from—as an owner, a family member, or part of the business—when they (or you) approach a problem or issue. That will lead to more productive engagement. If you're a founder of a business, and one child works with you while your other one lives across the country, you can understand their different viewpoints—that your child in the business might have the perspective of someone who's thinking about the nitty-gritty, whereas your other child may see things only for the perspective of how the business affects your family. You'll be able to see why one is interested in some things and ignores other things that might be of great interest to you or your child that is involved with the business.

Let's say the business buys your child a car because they are in sales and constantly on the road. That makes sense from the business perspective, but your other child might think it's unfair because their sibling gets a car and they don't—even though they don't work in the business. Once you understand that perspective, you're better equipped to have good communication. After all, how are you going to solve a problem if you don't understand what everybody is thinking? Each child is looking at it with a different point of view. *They got a car and I didn't.* They see it as a family perk, not a business perk.

Once everyone understands that there are different perks whether you are a family member (great family vacations), working in a business (company car), or an owner (dividends), it will fall into place. If one child works for a national firm and gets a company car, no one assumes they are being favoured and their siblings should also get one. But that's what can happen in a family business. The tension of family conflict is already starting, and you didn't realize it.

Each circle has its own perks, and when they overlap, it may not seem fair to others who are not in the circle and don't understand the dynamics of each circle. This is why communication is so important. Having that open and honest communication and understanding each other is so important to maintaining family peace and harmony. Using a Kolbe and/or PRINT® is a great starting point, as discussed earlier in this chapter.

These lenses are the foundation of good communication, and good communication is the foundation of everything else good that we work toward with our clients. Most families don't do a good job communicating about their business. Not between owners, not with other family members, not with their employees. Understanding these perspectives in the circles is a first step toward changing that.

Understanding these circles and their perspectives doesn't happen overnight, but it does happen, and you can achieve a very good outcome for yourself, your business, and your family with this understanding, even if starting is difficult. Just get the ball rolling. We are all procrastinators with some things, understand that, push through it, and get going. You will be glad you did.

We will go over in detail each of the three circles in the next few chapters. However, to get you thinking about your issues and what circle they fall into, we have some success questions to help build your understanding of your three circles. Not every question will be relevant to you, but the answers will help you build structure within your family and business that will assist in your succession planning. The more structure you have, the easier it will be to transition or sell.

Most of the questions you probably have the answers for, but they may need to be communicated with others and written down. No one can read your mind, so I have been told.

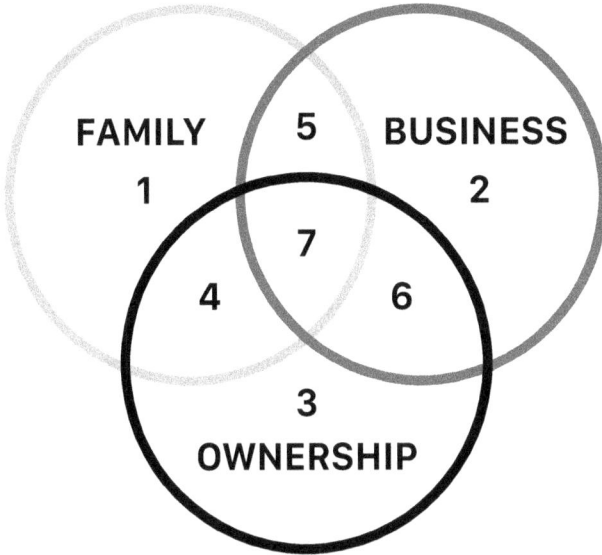

Fill in this blank three-circle model to identify the key members of your family and business.

1 . ...
2. ....
3. ....
4. ....
5. ....
6. ....
7. ....

With those circles thoughtfully filled in, you should now begin to see your pain points. Are you primarily dealing with a family issue, a business issue, or an ownership issue?

SUCCESS QUESTIONS

We've provided the following questions to start you thinking. Not every question will be relevant to you—that's OK. Focus on the ones that matter. This will help you to break down your business and understand where you need help most. Use the space provided or grab a sheet of paper. Don't skip it.

As you read each one, think of someone asking you the question. What is the first answer that comes to mind? Write it down.

- Do you feel you can't talk to a member of your family without a conflict arising?
    - Who is that member(s)?
    - What button do they push?
    - What are their body language, tone, and words like?

- Have you sat down with that person and discussed what sets you off and why?

- Do you have systems of communication in the house?
    - Family calendar?
    - To-do lists?
    - Preferred method of contact (email, text, phone call when someone is out of the house)?

- Were these decisions made by you, general consensus, or compromise?

- Do you have regular family meetings to make sure everyone is current and on the same page for what is going on in the family and the business?

- How is important information disseminated to family members? Who oversees keeping everyone in the loop?

- Is it time to sit down and reevaluate your communication strategy within the family, including spouses?

- What are the three circles of the Family Business Model?

Use your answers to begin to open the lines of communication. This allows everyone to get on the same page and prevents avoidances and conflict in all aspects of business and family.

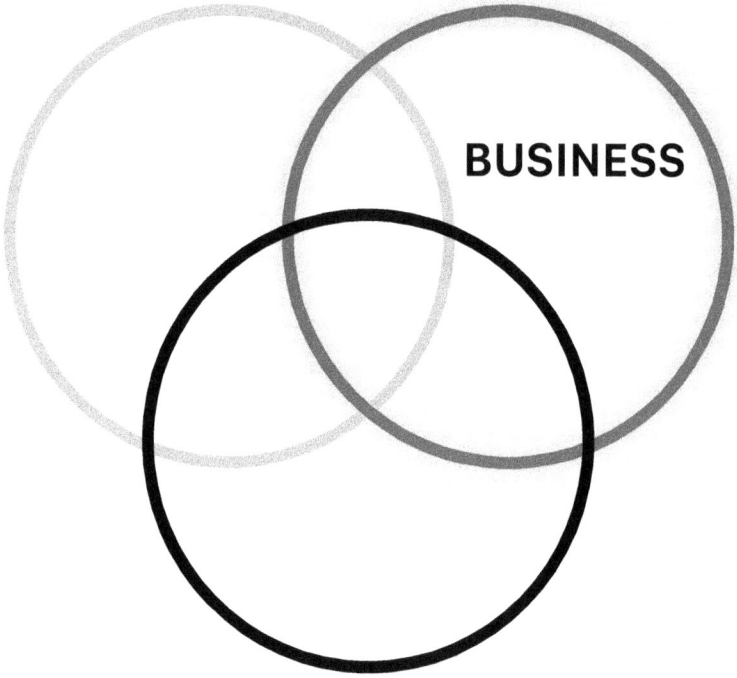

BUSINESS

CHAPTER 3

THE BUSINESS CIRCLE

"Great things in business are never done by one person;
they're done by a team of people."
—STEVE JOBS, American business magnate and inventor

The lines are very blurry between ownership and business in a first-generation business. As a business evolves and moves from generation to generation the systems and understanding of transition are clearer since the business and family have more experience. However, that first transition is the hardest, as you have nothing to base it on.

In the ownership circle you should be concerned with ownership issues. In the business circle you should be concerned with the management of the business. As an owner–operator you will likely have a role in the business that you are paid a salary for like any other employee. As a first-generation business either the ownership or family circle will give direction to the management of the business. It is management's role to follow the vision and direction that has been given.

Teamwork is imperative in the success and stability of your business. A strong team working with you at every level sets the foundation for success. You may need to start at the beginning, clarifying your values, your vision, your goals with your management team. When your management team is clear and on board they can ensure everyone on your team is as well. It will be easy for your management team to do their jobs well and with purpose if they know the vision for the company. Having everyone on board rowing in the same direction is a step toward being a self-reliant company. That's exciting for everyone. It sets you up for success and growth, strengthens your team, and prepares you for a smooth transition. It fosters pride and relief when you develop clarity around the vision and goals of the business. You are helping your team members think about the business as a whole.

If it seems overwhelming and too big a task to outline your values, vision, and goals on your own, engage your management team to help you. Have a vision-building day. Take your family values as your starting point. They will overlap with your business since you are the founder.

You will probably have some idea of your vision and goals from your ownership circle but may need help getting them on paper and executed for the business. Once you have identified where you want to go, your management will help you figure out what needs to be done to achieve what you have set out to do. That is the role of the business: to put in place and act on your vision and goals. Each member of your management team will take on their portion to move the goals forward.

> If it is processes and measuring your progress that you are struggling with, there are programs that can assist with setting up your office to be more systematized and get you on track to reach your goals. Not your client management system, but systems that help you simplify and achieve your goals. We use EOS® but there are others out there. If you want more information on EOS®, see the list of resources in the back of the book.

Does the Business Have Core Values?

Core values are different from vision. A vision is about where you're going. Core values define who you are and what you stand for. Core values are what your company was built on and they will never change. It is just who you are. Oftentimes small business owners aren't intentional with their core values. The business has them, it's just that no one has articulated them or written them down.

I realized that we had core values all along; I just didn't know what they were until we did an exercise for a marketing plan. This takes some time and thought, but your values will come out if you spend time with your leadership team and work on it.

Often your business core values are similar to your personal ones. Mainly because you started the company and work within your core values. Maybe that is why you left your previous employer—they didn't share your core values. Hmmmm, think about that. Maybe they were commission driven like my employer was, not need driven, or they don't care about the employees. There was a reason you left, and it was probably core values and you didn't know it. If you don't know what your core values are, here's a quick exercise to help you. Go to your boardroom or an off-site location with your leadership team. The number of people doesn't matter; it can be two or three people, your leadership team or employees who have been working with you for a while. They know you and the business. Use a flip chart or white-board and ask the following questions to everyone in the room and start writing. Write whatever comes to mind; don't think about it, just write it down.

- What made you successful when you started out in business?

- Why did your customers call you back?

- What positive feedback did you receive?

- What are some qualities people use to describe you?

- Look at your best current and past employees. What qualities or characteristics did they possess? Why were they your best employees?

Now that you have answered those questions and you have a few pages or a board full of words and phrases, do as follows:

- Circle the words that are repeated.

- Make a list of your circled words on a new page or section of the whiteboard.

- Group the words that have similar meanings together, words that say the same thing in different ways. You will probably end up with four to seven groupings of words.

- Pick a word that best describes that group of words. You might have to haul out the thesaurus. I have one bookmarked on my favorites bar.

Ta-da! These four to seven words are your core values. You've always had them; you just didn't name them. They have always been who you are as a company, and they will never change moving forward.

Now make sure everyone in the company knows them.

I start every team meeting writing down our core values. Then I ask for examples of what we have done since our last meeting that shone a light on our core values.

Each of my companies has their own core values, and they define me and the business:

HRSP:

- Helps First

- Relationships Matter

- Solutions Focused

- Progressive

SUCCESS:

- Solutions Focused

- Unique

- Caring

- Collaborative

- Educate

- Strategic

- Simplify

Although each company has different core values, they still reflect who we are and what we stand for as a company.

Is Your Vision, Long- and Short-Term, Clear?

If a tree falls in the forest does anybody hear? If your vision is not in writing, does anyone see it?

What is your vision for the next three, five, or ten years? Have you shared it with your family and employees? It is OK to dream big. If they don't know what your vison is, how can they participate in making it happen? How do you know if they are on board? How do you know if you are on track? You can't do it alone. You need support from every angle, Business, Family, and Ownership.

Vision is a huge part of a successful transition to the next generation. Get everyone on board. Your family may be very excited with your vision. I didn't think I was worthy of my vision, but after many years of keeping it inside I finally talked about it, and my family didn't think I was crazy. I was surprised. I pigeonholed myself. My bad.

If you've never thought about your vision before, let's start with breaking it down into two categories: the company vision and the vision for your role in the company.

Company Vision

Let's start easy. What is your vision for the company over the next three, five, or ten years? Is it profit, expansion, growth, change of target market? Once you have a vision, then you can think about what you need to do first to get the ball rolling.

Start by working backwards if you have a ten-year goal. Identify the goal, then think about where you should be in year five and year three to be on track. Based on where you are now, what can you realistically accomplish in one year to get on track toward your ultimate vision and goal?

Being overwhelmed is natural. I have done this many times. It is intimidating the first time. *Will they think I am crazy? Am I being overconfident?* When you have your leadership team in the room helping you, it will go much better than you expected. They get you and the company. If you are uncomfortable leading a meeting, recruit a trusted team or family member to stand up at the front of the room and lead the meeting.

Remember the elephant—one bite at a time. What is reasonable given your time frame? Having a vision doesn't mean you have to do all the work. With the right team you can get there. But you need to share your vision.

Do you have the right team to get the job done? Do you need to hire? Can you shift roles and responsibilities? Can you delegate? Kolbe, PRINT®, and EOS® could be useful tools to help build your team or shift the roles and responsibilities.

Once you know how a person handles tasks, you will know the right questions to ask to put them in the right roles. This makes it easier to shift roles and hire the right people for open positions. You can do it yourself, but there are tools that I have learned about and have shared in this book. I am so grateful to those people who have given me advice and guidance. It really does take a village! Until I had a business, I didn't really understand what that meant.

When you know what your vision is, and you can describe your vision to your team, you will ensure everybody is rowing in the same direction. Once you explain your vision, you may discover that not everyone on your team shares that view. Perhaps you are happy with your company's size, but you have relatives or employees who really want to be part of a bigger, growing enterprise. That's OK. Once you've laid out your vision, your employees can choose whether they want to be on the bus or off the bus. Either way, you'll have a better result.

What Is Your Vision for Your Role in the Company?

This may be the hardest role to visualize. You started it, grew it, it is your baby. *How can I leave it?* Do you know what role you want in the future?

You don't have to stop what you are doing; just think about if you could wipe the slate clean. What if you walked into the company today and could write your own job description? What would that role be? Duties, days per week, weeks off per year? What is your dream role? Mentor, sales, troubleshooter? How amazing would that be?

It doesn't have to be a dream. Now that you know what your dream role is, what is a realistic timeline to actually get you there? What can you start to do now or stop doing today, or what will take some time and planning? Where would you like to see yourself in one, five, and ten years? Have you talked to your leadership and family about your future role? How would you like your role to change, so you can focus on what you love in the business? This must be communicated to your family and team. They need to understand and share your vision.

Instead of making people nervous that you are making changes, if you communicate your thoughts and ideas, your team and family will see it as an opportunity to step up and grow in their own roles. You may be surprised at who may step up in both the business and the family to take a more active role.

Are Your Goals Written Down?

Goals are different from core values and vison. Values never change. Vision equals direction, the big picture. Goals are short term, what you need to accomplish to get to your vision, a stop along the way to achieve your long-term vision. For instance, "Our goal is to better track our clients' activities for better long-term communication." If everyone understands that's the goal, then it will make sense when you invest in a computer upgrade and software and ask your team to spend time cleaning up old files prior to the transition. Everybody gets it because they understand the goal and they have bought in. It makes it better for everyone in the company.

If you don't communicate your goals clearly, you might find it harder to implement changes. You need to communicate what's in your head! You may be the owner or founder, but you can't do what you want to do without talking about it.

Effective communication is important in all relationships, including in business, as mentioned earlier. No one can read your mind. That means having productive and informative meetings. In a small company, that could mean once a week or once a month over lunch. Talk about what needs to be addressed.

People are more likely to do what they're asked to do when they understand why and are engaged. Believe me. Thirty-eight years in business have taught me a lot. My hope is that you will take away at least one nugget from this book to help your family business be one of the 30 percent to pass on your success.

SUCCESS QUESTIONS

The following questions are meant for you to start thinking about vision, values, and goals. Not every question will be relevant to you—that's OK. Focus on the ones that matter. This will help you to break down your business and understand where you need help most. Use the space provided or grab a sheet of paper. Don't skip it.

As you read each one, think of someone asking you the question. What is the first answer that comes to mind? Write it down.

- Does the business have core values?

- Is your vision, both long- and short-term, clear?

- What is your vision for your role in the company?

- Are your goals written down?

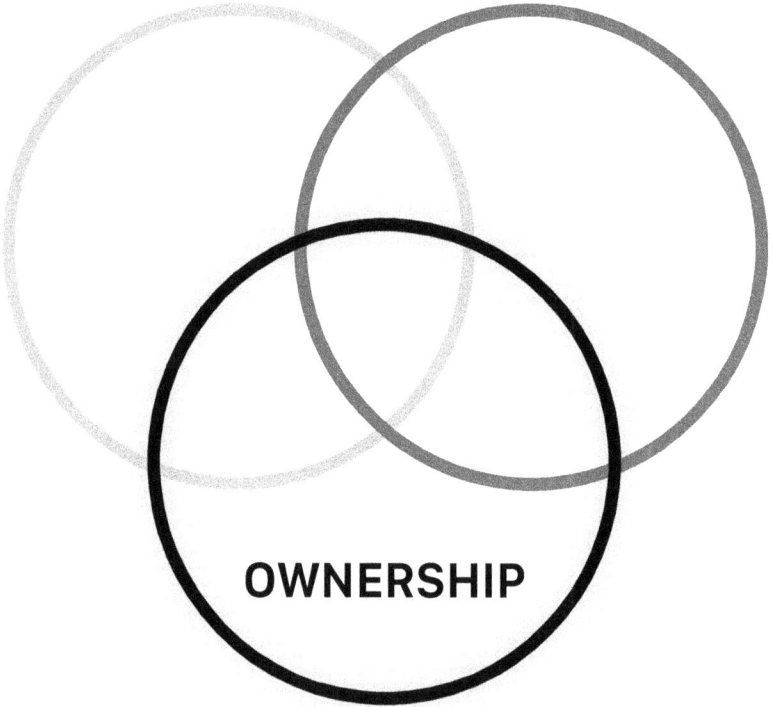

CHAPTER 4

THE OWNERSHIP CIRCLE

"You have family-owned businesses that have been around for five hundred years. You cannot name a corporation that survives intact for even a few decades."
—NASSIM NICHOLAS TALEB, Lebanese-American Essayist

Ownership in a first-generation family business is not as cut-and-dried as in other types of businesses. It takes open communication with your family to develop a plan for succession or transition of ownership, whatever the future ownership looks like in your family business.

The way to think about ownership is to remember that it's really about governance—that is, setting the direction for the management, marketability, and profit of the business. Owners set the course for the company. They have the big-picture vision, and they set the rules and policies that guide and control the business. It is leadership at its highest level. As a family business, you do this alone most of the time. Part of your role is setting up the company for success, by balancing the interests of the family and the business, keeping the business focused, and planning for events that are sometimes out of your control. One role as an owner is to plan for who should/could be the future owners. And how do you decide that?

I know as a first-generation business owner you have not been focused on ownership, but rather on running the business and supporting your family. That is very common before a first transition. Let's start with some basics.

How Do You Want to Bring the Next Generation into the Ownership of the Business?

Succession or transition planning from an ownership standpoint often gets pushed to the back burner. Too many factors and personalities at play. Easier to keep your head down and keep working *in* the business instead of *on* the business.

Most of my clients at one time or another have not wanted their kids to follow in their footsteps. They struggled getting the business up and running and want something better for their children.

Just like parenthood, starting and running a business doesn't come with a manual. It is trial by fire. Some days it makes sense to sell the business rather than plan for a transition, and other days we lean toward wanting all our hard work to carry on, to be a legacy. We have worked hard, and we don't want it to just end.

There are many ways to bring family members into the ownership circle of your business. They can buy in, be gifted shares, or assume ownership because of a death.

If they are entitled to ownership or a job by birthright, they may not get the respect of someone who is hired because of their qualifications. It might make sense for a family member to go to business school, trade school, or get an advanced degree in the industry, and then come into a role they've trained for. Or to bring them in on a rotation by having them work in every department or role so they understand what people do and how the business works. Have them earn the right to ownership. Such an approach is likely to give you, and your employees, greater peace of mind.

Ownership transition by the death of generation one is common. In my experience, death as a trigger for a succession or transition plan is talked about frequently but is slow to be implemented.

Commonly, insurance may be purchased for this reason, and the topic comes up often, yet the full plan may not ever be applied. Communication is the common theme in this book—you need to let your family know your wishes and put a plan in place for a smooth transition after your death. Death is one of the certainties in life, along with taxes. You will have to talk about it at some point if you want to make the decisions instead of someone else.

The bulk of my first-generation clients will not pass their business to their spouse upon their death; generally the spouse is not working in the business or is not interested in taking over and running something that is out of their skill set. They have a career of their own and are quite happy to stay in that career.

If they plan to pass the company on, most will pass it to a child or children who work in the business. However, a financial issue arises if it passes directly to a child or children—where does the spouse then get money to live on if the business is bypassing the spouse?

The business is generally the largest financial asset and has usually been counted on to supplement retirement. The child must have the ability to buy the surviving parent out, if the business is not an outright gift. Not very often is it a gift when a spouse is still alive. This is where having a business will and a personal will is ideal. You can have proper insurance in place both inside and outside of the business to make for a smooth transition. A death is a very emotional time, so make sure your wishes are up to date and in writing. The advice of an experienced family business advisor can be invaluable in planning for such situations.

But what if you want a family member to become owner before you pass away? What is the plan? What triggers the ownership change? An estate freeze? Splitting the company? Is it a full ownership change, or does it happen over a set period of time? Is it based on the size of the business, the age of the family member, their experience? Do they need to be working in the business? Is it gifted, bought, or based on growth, and what are the parameters? What about other children and stepchildren? Is everyone treated equally or fairly?

Family meetings are a good place to start these discussions. Since you are generally the only owner at this point, you need more input to keep peace and harmony. As mentioned before, the lines between the circles can be blurry when you are a first-generation business.

Do you trust your kids to carry on what you built? Are they dependable? Do they know what they're doing? Do they really want to get into your industry? Are they interested in being in the business because they are passionate about it, or because it's an easy option? This can be tricky ground for parents, who tend to view their children as, well, children, even after they're fully fledged adults. A clear process for bringing the next generation into the business and handing over the reins will serve everyone involved.

Ask yourself what you want. You might say, "Well, I want to be fully out of the business in ten years." If you have family members who are interested in stepping in, consider where they are in their development. Are they still kids? Are they in school? What would they need to do for you to be able to exit in ten years? Maybe they need business skills. Or trade skills. Or time on the job.

Since you sit in the center of the three circles it is your responsibility to get these conversations started or to bring in the right advisors to help you start the conversations. Define what it takes to be a family member working in the business or owning the business. It is not a one-and-done conversation. It will take some time and guidance.

Once you've figured out what you want for yourself and your family members, turn your attention to your ownership options. There are multiple ways to be an owner in a business, and you might not have thought of all of them (more about this below). Shifting to a different type of ownership than your present involvement may be part of what you do in your succession plan.

Drawing Income from Your Business

Do you need to harvest the value of the business to retire? Or would you like to receive regular dividends from it? As you wear your ownership hat, think about how you want to get rid of or change your ownership, because that's what you are doing in the succession process.

What are the options available to you? Right now, you may be the only owner. What is going to change, how, and why? (You may answer many of these questions through family meetings, which we discuss in a later chapter.)

Many of the people we work with are surprised to learn that they can draw income from their business even if they're not working in it. First gens equate working in the business with owning and drawing income from the business. As long as you set things up correctly and ensure that your successors are able to run the company profitably, by building on what you created, you can have your cake and eat it too. This is often welcomed news. Too frequently, we meet families who think they have to sell their companies because the owners need the money and the second generation can't afford to buy their parents out.

For example, you may be interested in receiving dividends from the company as you shift from an active to a more passive role. Previously you may have relied on your salary and plowed dividends back into the business to grow it. The questions you'll ask in your new ownership role will change: *Do we have enough profits to pay out dividends? Do we need to grow? How are we going to do that? How are we ensuring we stay profitable? Are we following our values and goals as we do that?* With questions like these, you must be sure you have the right systems in place for accountability. Do you have systems and processes for the new operators—the people who take operations over from you—to follow, to consistently report to you, and to gather direction and feedback from you? Do you have policies in place that define the relationship between owners and between the owners and the business? Ownership is a governance role. Looking down at the business from above, setting the company up for success. Review the business circle to remind yourself of how important it is to have processes and get the company ready for transition or a sale.

Most of your assets are probably tied up in this business, so of course you want to make sure that the next generation continues to grow and maintain profitability. Accountability is a big part of doing just that. Clarity on relationships, and clarity on the way reporting and guidance work, will go a long way toward building trust as you hand off the company's reins.

Another way to remove money from your company is to consider whether you can divide it. Is there one part that a family member would really excel in, and another that you could sell off?

This is why you hold family meetings! You may never have had explicit conversations in your family—many families don't—about who can be in the business, who wants to be in the business, what it takes to be in the business, and what you, as the first generation, want to get out of the business. Open conversations, perhaps facilitated by a professional, are an essential part of succession planning. (More about this in Chapters 5 and 6.)

Three Types of Ownership

There are three different types of ownership that are particularly relevant for first- and second-generation business owners: operating, governing, and passive.

1. Most first-generation owners think of owning the business and working in the business as the same thing, but they are not. *Operating* owners are involved in the day-to-day operations of the business as employees. While employees of businesses receive a salary or hourly wage, and owners of businesses receive dividends, operating owners receive both—because they own the company, *and* they work in it every day. If your kids come into the business but don't yet have ownership stakes, they're not operating owners. They're simply employees.

2. *Governing* owners oversee the business and are often engaged in directing it but are not employees. They operate like board members, setting policies and procedures and direction. This can be a very productive role for a first-generation owner to move into as the second generation becomes operating owners. The first

generation can still be involved in a valuable way. They can use their experience and wisdom to make sure the business stays on track as they gain trust in the next generation's abilities. Governing owners receive dividends but no salary. A nice transition.

3. *Passive* owners are not involved in the vision or direction of the business but do collect dividends. If you can let go, this is ideal!

Now that you have a basic understanding of the three types of ownership, you can figure out the next step in your transition plan. It is not an all-or-nothing shift.

Who Can Be an Owner?

One role of those in the ownership circle is to make sure there are no accidental owners. I encountered a situation where a founder passed suddenly, and his twenty-year-old son, who was completely unprepared, inherited the company. Nobody saw this coming, and everything—the success of the business, the owner's surviving spouse's security, his son's career—was at risk. This situation was a product of previous decisions that were both fear based and love based, rather than being rational and well thought out.

Too many owners, especially first-generation owners, make decisions out of fear or love. They make decisions because they don't want to lose control, or they don't want to hurt someone's feelings. They don't want to pit one child against another. They tell themselves, "I want my kids to be treated equally, so I'm going to do X"—like divide ownership equally between siblings regardless of what their children want or their capabilities. That might not be the best choice. Such owners avoid difficult conversations. They do their succession planning—if they do it at all—on their own, and the results can be a nightmare. They might have the best of intentions, but they often get the worst results. This goes back to the foundation of communication. Without it, it's anyone's guess as to what you are thinking.

So, who can or should be an owner? It's not a simple question. Should ownership be limited to bloodline only? What about in-laws? Stepchildren? Outside management? In my family, at the moment, ownership would continue down the bloodline; my sons and grand-children can be owners. This may change over time as the business grows and develops. That is the wonderful part of being a family-run business. You can change direction in a heartbeat.

Do You Regularly Talk about Succession with Your Family?

Complacency is not good. It's never too early to have important dis-cussions with your family—not only for the first generation, but also for the second generation. Founders are thinking about how they want to transition out of the business; the next generation should be thinking carefully about if, and how, they want to get into the busi-ness. Even if you're just starting out, have conversations with your family about ownership and structure. Having the right people in the right seats is important—the next generation should have the ben-efit of coming into a business that is thriving with structure in place.

Time and again I've seen first-generation companies that are doing well and providing the owner a good income, but when the owner steps back a bit the business begins to slide because there's nobody clearly in charge. They haven't set the next generation or the business up for success. They think, *We're doing well. Rather than sell the business or come up with a plan for succession, we're just going to let it run on autopilot.* But without the proper mechanisms in place for transparency and accountability, the business can deteriorate. When a business is new, you don't take your eye off the ball—so don't do that when it is mature, and you are ready to step back. This comes back to governance, which includes good communication and clear decision-making, including with all stakeholders.

Can the Business Support Your Succession Plans?

Succession often brings up questions of growth. Do you need to grow the business to take dividends from it and support the people who took over your roles? Do you need to grow it to sell it for the price you need?

Think of it from a different standpoint—not considering only what you can take from the business, but asking how the business needs to grow to maintain your lifestyle. Now, how are you going to get it there? This, again, is an ownership issue in the business. How can you grow the business to what you need it to be? Think outside the box. Should you buy another business, develop a new market, use tools to streamline? Should you cull your lower revenue streams or clients, using the 80/20 rule of business (the top 20 percent of your clients generate 80 percent of your revenue)? Should you add a new product line to your business? How can you grow the business without doubling your employees' workload?

Give your mandate to your leadership team and let them brainstorm ideas. Work together to develop a plan to get there. The longer your runway to succession, the more likely you will be successful.

Don't be afraid of making necessary changes to create the growth that will support your new ownership role and the next generation.

SUCCESS QUESTIONS

The following questions are designed to get you thinking about the various aspects of the ownership circle. Not every question will be relevant to you—that's OK. Focus on the ones that matter. This will help you to break down your business and understand where you need help most. Use the space provided or grab a sheet of paper. Don't skip it.

As you read each one, think of someone asking you the question. What is the first answer that comes to mind? Write it down.

- How do you want to bring the next generation into the ownership of the business?

- Are you aware of the different types of ownership?

- Is ownership versus working in the business clear to you, your family, and your employees?

- Who can be an owner (consider stepchildren, in-laws, key employees)?

- Do you talk regularly about transition or succession with your family?

- Can the business support your succession plans?

Most of these conversations should be held in a family meeting and/or with your family business advisors. Make sure you get the answers you need to these questions before making decisions you can't reverse. These questions take a lot of thought and discussion, and the key is to keep the conversations going. Don't put them on the back burner.

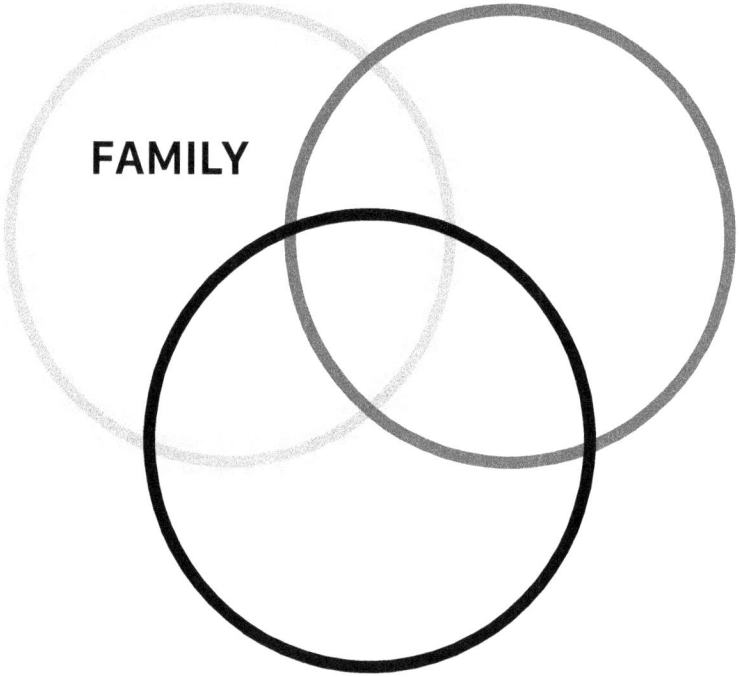

FAMILY

CHAPTER 5

THE FAMILY CIRCLE

"In modern use family may refer to one of several different groups of people or things collectively, such as chemical compounds, related languages, plants and animals, and people who may or may not share ancestry. Family is often encountered in legal use, but even within the jargon of the law it is not restricted to a single meaning. In many legal contexts family denotes 'individuals related by blood, marriage, or adoption,' but in others the definition may be somewhat broader, encompassing groups of individuals not related by these things."
—MERRIAM-WEBSTER DICTIONARY

Each family is as unique as each family business. Traditions, expectations, and style of communication are unique to each, from how they deal with grief to how they make decisions. There is no simple answer on how to deal with all the issues that surround a family and particularly one that owns a business.

The family guides and drives the direction of business depending on what the family needs or wants from the business. Each family member, depending on where they sit in the three-circle model, may have a different want or need and look at decisions from their singular perspective only. Your responsibility, as the one who sits in the middle where all the circles intersect, is to help your family members understand the other angles and perspectives. Help them see the entire picture and fill in what they didn't know they were missing.

Common Challenges in the Family

Getting the conversations going requires families to overcome some challenges. Every family has its challenges; most of the time it is easier to avoid them than to hit them head-on. I have not seen a study on this, but I assume the percentage is quite high when looking at families that have avoided a conversation or not brought up an issue because the topic was uncomfortable. And when it was finally tackled, it was not as bad as they thought, or they made it worse by avoiding it for too long. Either way, it is not going away, so back to Nike—it is time to . . . *just do it!*

I have outlined several challenges that I have run into over my career. The goal is to be aware of these challenges and find a way to overcome them or start the conversation to work toward finding a solution.

Fear of Change

One problem I see in family businesses is fear of change. The first generation is accustomed to doing things a certain way. They can be closed-minded to exploring new ideas. What they have been doing has worked well, so why change anything now? They may also have not had the time to really think about making changes as they were working *in* the business, not *on* the business. They don't want to do anything that could threaten the stability of the business.

Fear of Conflict

I worked with one family in which the mom could not handle any kind of conflict. All she wanted was for her kids to get along and be happy. She didn't want anyone upset and as a result would not let any hard conversations happen. But that made it incredibly difficult to understand the true issues and work through them. We did come up with a solution on how to deal with perceived conflict after a few meetings, and now each meeting is more productive than the last.

In my experience, this isn't too uncommon in a first-generation business. The mom is often the head of the family and the family circle, and she wants to ensure there's never conflict between her children; she wants to be able to have dinner with everyone together. She wants everybody to be treated equally. But there is a big difference between fair and equal. Family meetings can help determine what "fair" means.

The Loud Voice Dominates

I often see that whoever leads the business tends to jump in and lead the family meeting, dominating it. Many people think that the business is controlled by the person who founded it, and so that person is allowed to have the most say. In a family meeting, that's not true. If that happens, it's not a family meeting anymore.

With the dominate person running the family meetings, it may be challenging for other family members to feel like they will be heard. Many times, they shut down and say nothing.

No Experience with Succession Planning

Working on succession from first generation to second can be challenging, because the family hasn't yet transitioned a business. By the time the third generation gets involved, a family usually has the basics of a plan and a system for passing the business from one generation to the next. But the first time around there is no history to guide you. That's why you need to put in the time and energy to think about what you want, communicate well, and build something equitable and durable. Seek help.

Sibling Rivalry

I frequently see sibling rivalries at play in family meetings. I see entitlement come out, when one child feels they deserve something that another has or wants. When family members work in the business, they can think, *Hey, I worked on this for years and my brother didn't, so why should he get any of it?* That can create real conflict.

Start the conversations early. What are the parameters for working in the business? Make sure everyone knows what it takes to be a leader or an employee. Is it education, experience, level of comfort? Embrace the differences in your children. Having family meetings lets them learn to work together to make decisions. The business is just one asset in your estate; don't let your family assume what is going to happen, and don't assume you know how your children feel.

Money Discomfort

Don't like talking about money? Remember that you can't take it with you, and you only have three choices about where it's going to go: to your kids, to charity, or to Revenue Canada. You must talk about it. What better place than at a family meeting?

Underestimating Your Kids

A big challenge is the ability to see your grown children as adults. If you still see them as your kids, it prevents you from appreciating their input and stifles their voice. The family meeting is a critical opportunity to let them be heard and seen for who they are, not who you think they are.

The hardest part of a family business is getting it going and making it last long enough to have something to pass on. The next generation was born at a different time and has new, fresh ideas or different skill sets based on experience or education. They are not you and never will be. Personalities are a big part of transitions. See them for who they have become.

Protecting Your Family

Many of the founders we work with discourage their children from joining the business. They remember how hard the first years were, how much they had to work to build it, and how they didn't have much to show for a long time. Now that it is established, the business has to deal with ongoing industry or economic challenges. Many parents don't want their kids to have to deal with that. They think it will be easier somewhere else. I am here to tell you the grass is not always greener. Every business has its own challenges and limitations. This limited view will prevent you from giving your children other opportunities in the business, such as management, marketing, sales, or office roles.

You may think you're protecting them by having them work somewhere else, but why waste all your hard work? Give them an opportunity.

In-Laws

A few of the problems I have come across in family business are in-stigated by outsiders, meaning in-laws. They haven't grown up in the family, and they don't understand the family and its traditions and values. They don't understand why you are the way you are.

Remember, they have the ear of your child who is listening to them like they used to listen to you. You are not as influential as you once were. Family meetings are a good way to bridge that gap and educate the in-laws. Embrace them; don't alienate them.

Personalities

Many challenges and conflicts are based on the differences in peo-ple's personalities and why people react the way they do. We think everyone should be the same as we are. They should think, feel, and do things just like we do. We get upset and don't understand why they are like they are. Especially our kids.

As a business we have our team leaders do different indexes to get a better understanding of their thinking, feeling, and doing (the three parts of the brain discussed in the communications chapter). Why don't we do that with our family? We want to understand our team so we can communicate better and avoid conflicts at work, so why not at home too?

Once we introduced PRINT® and Kolbe to our family clients it was a game changer. It is the first thing we do now. Understanding the unconscious motivators that are responsible for thoughts, feelings, and actions of your family members makes it clear why they react the way they do, with no surprises. Understanding how they make deci-sions and start projects sets the stage for making better decisions and choices. Less friction and stress.

Stronger family transfers to a stronger business.

Estate Planning as a Family

I ask clients all the time, "If you had to give away all of your assets today, where would they go?" Then I ask, "If I asked you this five years ago, would it have been different from today?" It almost always would be different, because things change. Someone is going to decide what happens to your money and assets, so shouldn't it be you, when you are calm, are healthy, and can plan? Plans that you make today are not cast in stone; you can make changes as your situation requires. What matters is setting up the basics, having the foundation in place and having open conversations with your family.

The discussion and the planning should be around your total wealth, not just the business. You will have other assets to deal with, such as property, or deferred assets like RRSPs, or valuables such as artwork. You have assets and you can't take them with you. Where are they going to go? Is everything going to charity? Do the kids get it? Is there a split between children? Are you setting up trusts? Within your estate, the family business is likely the driver that creates the money and wealth, so naturally its disposition is a big question worthy of serious attention. But it's not the only one.

There are many ways to create fairness around the division of assets among family members, and that's an important thing to strive for. Fair versus equal. One of you is trying to be equal, while the other one wants it to be fair. What is your family's definition and stance on it? As part of the estate planning process, you must think about who wants what, and who is prepared and capable at this point. Obviously, this is not an easy or quick decision. It will take some time and perhaps some difficult conversations.

Estate planning is more than just having a will and some life insurance. It requires some serious thought about your legacy. It can also be complicated by second marriages and stepchildren.

You probably never thought you would be in this position, worrying about estate planning. You started your company years ago so you could have an income. Now it is time to think about your legacy and how to protect your family, today and for future generations.

Hiring Family Members

Making the decision to hire family members is a tough one. And it is usually decided at the family-circle level. It is a topic that is not generally addressed at the first-generation level until an issue comes up. Remember, family members can extend past your kids to cousins, nieces, nephews-in-law. The rules should be the same for everyone so as not to cause a family feud. You love your niece, hired her, and made a role for her. However, you don't feel the same about your nephew. How is that going to go over!

If they are blood relatives, does that mean they have special priorities or perks? Even if they are entitled to a job through birthright, should they be qualified and adhere to the same rules as everyone else? Must they do the job well? Can they be fired? Do they get the same pay as everyone else in that role? Setting the parameters for family will avoid conflict and resentment later.

Any family members working in the business must be mindful of the hats they wear too. If a family member overrides a decision, are they doing that because they think they're special and get special treatment? Or because the process doesn't work for everyone? If the process doesn't work, fix it.

If a family member thinks things should be different for them, that's not going to fly. Your processes have to be the same for everyone. Yes, family members may get additional benefits because they are family members, but those are separate from their roles as employees and must be kept separate.

This is essential not only for your day-to-day culture, but it's also important if you are grooming a family member to take over from you. Someday this young woman or young man may be the boss. They will succeed in that role only if they have proven themselves in the eyes of everyone who works in your family business. Set them up for success by having them earn the respect of the others in the business. Great family meeting topic. Decide before an issue comes up.

SUCCESS QUESTIONS

I have provided some questions for you to start thinking about your family circle. Not every question will be relevant to you—that's OK. Focus on the ones that matter. This will help you to break down your business and understand where you need help most. Use the space provided or grab a sheet of paper. Don't skip it.

As you read each one, think of someone asking you the question. What is the first answer that comes to mind? Write it down.

- Are there any topics that are taboo in your family?

- Who is entitled to a job?

- What challenges to open and honest conversations do you have in your family?
    - Fear of change?
    - Fear of conflict?
    - In-laws?
    - Loud voice dominating?
    - Personalities?
    - Money discomfort?
    - Underestimating your kids?
    - Protecting your children?

- Do you have an up-to-date will? Business and personal?

- If you had to give everything away today, where and to whom would it go?

Have you discussed estate planning with your family?

Now that you've read a detailed description about each of the three circles in the Family Business Model, consider the following questions. Your answers will bring you to a solid understanding of how your unique dynamic works.

Business Circle

- Can the business financially support your succession or transition plan?

- Do you have office processes documented?

- Could you hand off your business today without issue?

- Do you have a strong leadership team you can rely on?

- Are you doing multiple roles in the business?

- Do you have the correct employees in the correct roles?

- Is the company financially sound?

Ownership Circle

- Have you thought about if and how to bring the next generation into the ownership of the business?

- Have you thought about who could be an owner in the future (stepchildren, in-laws, key employees)?

- Are you thinking of selling or gifting shares?

- Are you aware of the different types of ownership available to you?

- Would you like to maintain some ownership long term?

- Is the difference between the roles and responsibilities of ownership versus working in the business clear?

Family Circle

- Do you talk regularly about retirement and transition or succession with your family?

- Do you hold family meetings with specific topics on the agenda?

- Is everyone in the family on the same page in terms of charitable giving, employment, and legacy?

- Is there a plan for family members to be part of the business? Working or ownership?

- Does the family know the long- and short-term vision of the company?

- Is employment in the business considered a birthright? What about for stepchildren?

- Do family members understand the impact the business has in the community?

- Do family members know the plan moving forward if a parent dies or becomes disabled?

- Do you have a plan for generational wealth transfer (estate planning)?

CHAPTER 6

THE FAMILY MEETING

"The family meeting, a surprisingly powerful tool to get your kids engaged."
—DR. ALISON ESCALANTE, Pediatrician and Adjunct Professor of Pediatrics
at Rush University

In my experience, the best way to get everyone on the same page so you will not be accused of "you didn't tell me that" is to have a family meeting. A family meeting is not a confrontation or a discussion at the dinner table; a family meeting is similar to how you would hold a business meeting at work. Everyone is in the same room, you have an agenda, you get to bring up the issues to everyone at the same time, and everyone has an opportunity to speak and be heard. No one is left out.

If only it was that easy. I can tell you it is not. You have a million excuses for not having family meetings, you don't have time, everyone's schedule is all over the place, kids' activities, work, social commitments—you name it, there is a reason to avoid it. Not to mention, you are not sure why you should or how you would hold a family meeting. Generally, when a family meeting is called it is to share bad news, and no one wants bad news. This is your opportunity to change that, call the first one, and make it informative and positive.

Family meetings are another form of communication. The reason many families don't communicate well is because it's hard! You may need to have conversations you never have had or you don't want to have. When you start having these conversations, you're likely to raise issues, questions, and assumptions that are not only surprising to you but to other family members as well. They're surprising because you haven't talked about them before. Instead, people have been making assumptions. For example, a founder might discover that his child secretly wanted to work in the business but was never invited in; they didn't feel they had the right skills or had an oil and vinegar relationship with their parent, so they moved across the country and started a new life. There can be a lot of emotion around these conversations, which can become quite challenging. We offer more guidance on how to manage these conversations a bit later.

Once you have had or begin to have those conversations, you can start to clear the air. Coming to a shared understanding can be very difficult at first, but over time—sometimes a lot of time—you begin to get acceptance for a larger vision and plan for the future of your family and your business. The interests of the family, the owners, and the business will line up, and everyone involved (if you do this right) will be on the same page, maybe for the first time. This is better for everyone. The business becomes less stressful for those involved. It runs better, generating more wealth and income. You come together as a family.

Transition or succession planning revolves around the family unit. Communicating your thoughts and plans to the entire family is important. If you are looking to slow down or sell, you should engage the entire family so you don't miss something you should have seen or asked about earlier. Talking about it and getting input from all sides is a great way to confirm your decision and get the support you need to make the changes. I am not talking about dinner table meetings, but planned meetings with an agenda. Consider it a same-page meeting like you would have at work. All stakeholders at the same table.

If all parties are around the table at the meeting listening and joining in the discussion, it can still turn out like the telephone game we played as kids. One person whispers a story into another person's ear, they repeat it into the next person's ear, and on and on it goes around the circle. At the end when the last person repeats it out loud, the story is nowhere near what it started out as. That happens every day in real life—*how many times have you said, that is not what I said, it was taken out of context, or I didn't say that at all, what I meant was . . .* you get it.

The goal of the very first family meeting is to educate and to align. Start with the purpose of the meeting: Why are we here? Explain why you want to start having meetings. It is hard to have important discussions with people in different locations. Who do you tell first? The best outcome is having everyone in the same room at the same time.

Remember, you are holding this meeting because as a family you need to be on the same page. Everyone should understand what is at stake and have the opportunity to discuss how they are feeling about the issue. Optimally, you come out of the meeting aligned as a family. If you don't achieve that right away, don't worry—now you at least know what you need to keep working on. Family meetings are not one-and-done events. Just as you don't have one management meeting in your company and never meet again, you don't have one family meeting and call it done. You will be surprised what comes out at the first meeting.

A family meeting does not have to be dull—it could be a weekend away, just the family, to share some fun and discuss the business. A long weekend away with half a day dealing with family and business issues. Your family, your meeting.

There are four cornerstones to building your family meetings.

1. Family development (learning, future planning)

2. Family cohesion (vision, values, hopes, and dreams)

3. Family business and assets (information sharing, brainstorming about the business)

4. Family fun (games, travel, fun activities)

A family meeting starts with dedicated time. A family meeting is about sharing information. Without open and honest conversations, people fall into unspoken assumptions. Dad might think, *Well, I founded it, my son works in it now, so it should go to him.* But Mom might think, *I want to make sure everyone is treated equitably, so we have to divide it between all three kids.* Or both parents assume there is no way their children can afford to buy the business from them, so selling to an outsider is the only way for them to withdraw their wealth from it. Or they don't feel their kids are properly prepared to take the business on, so there's no point in even discussing it. These all make for great family discussions.

Several of my families were shocked when their assumptions were untrue. They just assumed the kids didn't want the business because of some off-the-cuff comments about the business—when in fact the kids did want the business, just not in the shape it was currently in, and they didn't feel they would be heard or taken seriously if they made suggestions.

Family business finances is another taboo topic but should not be kept a secret. Believe me, your family knows that you're either making money or losing money. That comes with the territory of owning a business, so there is no reason to hide the details from the people who are affected by it. You must talk openly and honestly with each other, and family meetings are the place to start. Nobody wants tension at the dining room table, so move those topics to the family meeting. You don't have to get into the nitty-gritty to begin with and talk about how the business is doing financially. Every business has its ups and downs. Does your family know how the economy or lack of qualified trades is impacting your bottom line? Maybe you can brainstorm options. Be open and honest.

It is never too late or too early to start your family meetings. When our two boys were little, we had meetings to discuss our charitable donations. Our kids learned that we give back—that doing so is a family value, and the business is an extension of the family that allows us to live that value. It represents us. That was an important lesson for them to grasp. Without the business, we would not be in a position to give back as much as we do. They began to realize that the business is not only important to the family but to the community. It, like the family, has a reputation that needs nurturing and protecting.

If you're still uncertain about the value of family meetings, ask yourself these questions:

- Has a transition or retirement plan been discussed with family members?

- Is there a plan for family members to be part of the business?

- Have you asked if any family members are interested in being involved in the business?

- Do all family members know the plan moving forward if a parent dies or becomes disabled?

- Have you discussed who can be a future owner of the business?

- Is the family engaged in the vision of the company or only peripherally involved?

- Is employment in the business considered a birthright?

- Do all family members understand the impact the business has in the community?

If you're like most first-generation families who have a business, your answers to these questions will not always be yes. Family meetings can get you to yes or at least to a consensus.

As the conversations open up (over multiple meetings), you can discuss anything that is relevant and/or timely, like succession, compensation, family values, company history, responsibility to the community and employees, company vision, family wealth, decision-making, and ownership. These discussions lead to conversations about options.

As I have mentioned, most founders don't even know what their succession options are—they assume they work in their business, or they sell it. A family business planning professional with a broader scope of experience can help you understand your choices, but you still have to start by talking to each other. If you are concerned about what to start with, just start with the basics as mentioned before. Or begin by getting your Kolbe and PRINT® tests done as a family, so you can begin to truly understand each other.

How to Begin the Family Meeting

Well, remember you are holding a meeting because there is an issue (or ten) to address. If you hit those issues at a dead run, you're probably not going to get the result that you want. But if you take it slow, one bite at a time, and get everyone on the same page, you'll get a solution that everyone agrees to.

When you first introduce the idea of holding a family meeting, you can say something like, "It's important that we get together and talk a little bit about estate planning, including the business. We want to talk about the future and get everyone's input. We're going to do it off-site. We'll take half a day and talk about where Mom and Dad are going in our lives. We'll talk about the business and what it does for the family, and what we're trying to do with it, so everybody has a similar understanding and has a chance to weigh in. When we are done, we can have a nice lunch." Or something along those lines. Very casual and comfortable. That approach should set them at ease and encourage engagement.

Once you have the meeting set, remember the first family meeting is about three things:

- Getting everybody to understand some basic facts and appreciate the openness.

- Encouraging people to be engaged and to want to participate in future meetings.

- Showing that there's value in these meetings.

At or prior to the meeting, go back to the three circles: owner, business, family. Draw them out on a piece of paper or a whiteboard and place your family members where they belong in the diagram. This simple diagram creates a strong visual aid to help everyone in the family see how different people view the business and may approach questions about it. Review the three-circle model with them and encourage them to use it as a reminder of what lens they're using when they approach a question or problem.

Rules of Thumb for Successful Family Meetings

This can be set as an agenda at your first meeting:

- Choose someone who will chair the meetings (if not using a facilitator).

- Choose someone who arranges the meetings and logistics.

- Choose a note taker, who then sends out the notes and manages the follow-ups, if any.

- Set the rules for all meetings:
  - Cell phone rules.
  - How to settle arguments.
  - How to ensure everyone is heard and has a chance to speak.
  - Update the rules as necessary.

- Decide how often you will meet.

- Decide how the agenda for the next meeting is set.

You get the idea. This is your family and your meeting. You choose the agenda based on your family's needs. However, it needs structure for it to be productive—it needs a start time and end time and everyone's buy-in. It can't be a waste of time, or it will lose its value.

I have our families bring out the rules and set them on the table for the first few meetings as a reminder. One page, big font!

Pre-Meeting Questionnaire

Meetings are most productive when people show up prepared. If you've never held a family meeting, you may not even know what you need to talk about. Or you may think you know, but you're missing something important.

Before I facilitate the first meeting for a family, I interview each member individually. The list of questions I bring is preplanned with the family member who asked me to get involved. Each family member is asked the same questions. This gives me an opportunity to get their take on any issues, concerns, or questions they may have. From their answers, I build an agenda of items that should be addressed first.

You can do something similar by sending out a questionnaire. We have a whole host of questions to pull from, depending on why we were asked to help out. We regularly ask key people in the business a few questions as well to get an understanding and angle from all three circles. The business is an important element and certainly helps the family members decide what to add to the agenda for future meetings.

Have an Agenda and an Intention to Listen

Circulate an agenda for input prior to the meeting based on the questionnaire. Let everyone have a say on the agenda items. It's very important that family meetings be held in a safe environment, preferably a neutral place, where everyone can feel heard and not judged. Make sure everyone is heard before and during the meetings. You can use a roundtable method to ensure everyone is heard. No interrupting, let them finish. An example of a Family Meeting Agenda can be found at the end of this chapter.

Take It Slow

You don't have to start family meetings by talking about tough topics right away. I always start every meeting with a positive focus: tell me something positive that has happened in the last week, month, ninety days (depends on the last time we met). It gets you feeling good and those endorphins moving!

After the icebreaker, you can focus on the meeting etiquette, move on to the questionnaire, or lob an easy question: "Do you think as a family we are open and honest with each other?" Or you might begin by talking about what the business does—don't assume everyone knows. Say, "Let me tell you a little about the history of our business." This is important if you have stepchildren or in-laws at the meeting. Or you can share your vision or how you've planned your estate (or not!). Save that for a later meeting.

The conversations should not be about what anybody has done wrong (such as not communicating or not participating). They're about looking forward and seeking involvement and buy-in.

Use the questionnaire as a guideline once you get the housekeeping out of the way. You can have one person start with a question of their choosing and everyone goes around the table one by one and answers that question. Once everyone has had their say, the next person picks a question to answer, and again everyone has their say. This would continue until the last question has been discussed. You may not get to the end of the list by the meeting adjournment; that is OK, and you can continue at your next family meeting.

Some answers may spark tension, so you must have an agreed-upon solution to park that topic for another time or come to a mutually agreeable solution. You will develop new meeting etiquettes as you have more and more meetings—like a system for tiebreakers or the limit of time someone gets to talk, or when to call time-out to regroup or take a breather. This is your family and your rules.

If you haven't sent out the questionnaire, then you can get into questions like, "Does this business interest you? Would you like to be involved? How would you like to contribute?" Maybe you thought your kids want to take over from you, and you find out they don't. They aren't interested in the responsibility. That's good to know, isn't it? It certainly could change your plans. Come up with your questions for the first meeting, and after the first meeting the agendas will almost set themselves. Or something will have come up between meetings that someone will add to the agenda once they get used to the meetings and the structure.

If you've never discussed things like family values, you may need to take a while, hear from everyone, and come to agreement on that subject. Once values are clear you can talk about succession and how it could work. Succession is a complex subject with many possibilities, and of course every family is unique. The right solution for one family will not be right for another. When you start to discuss succession, the very first questions to ask can go like this:

- Is this a business we want to sell or keep in the family?

- Is it something that provides essential funds, and we need to keep it going?

- Is this business something that we are proud of and want to carry on?

- Could we split the business?

Try not to start any meeting with a tough topic. You can send out a questionnaire for each meeting if you find that easier. It is hard to facilitate your own meeting, so having the family prepared in advance will make it easier on you as the facilitator. You don't want to be seen as controlling the discussion or not allowing everyone to have their say.

When you are ready to talk about estate planning, you can start by asking your family members about their expectations. Ask, "What do you think is going to happen to the business/money when I die or retire?" It's a good way to see if everyone is on the same page and, if not, what needs to be addressed to get to that same page. You might have a child who doesn't care about the business, but they probably care about the estate! This topic could be its own questionnaire and take several meetings. These are not easy topics, hence the reason people shy away from them.

Facilitation

If you are facilitating your own meetings, it is important that the answers to the questions are not sent to a family member to analyze and summarize in advance of the meeting. You will not get honest answers if they know who will be reading their responses in advance.

In my company, we analyze and summarize, because we are a third party and don't have a vested interest in the answers. But if your family members know another family member is reading their responses, they will either not answer or they will tailor the responses to the reader, and you will not get their true, unfiltered responses. When we analyze the responses (we ask our questions over the phone; we find we get better responses than if we ask for them in writing), we are very careful to word the results so as not to put the spotlight on a specific family member. This is difficult for small families but very doable. It just takes time to craft the responses. If you are facilitating your meetings, have your family bring their answers to the meeting to be shared. Let them have their say in their own words.

Meet on Neutral Ground

Don't meet in your home if you can avoid it. Go somewhere you can focus and be uninterrupted. Have an agenda and follow it. Understand and respect what "circle" each person sits in.

Meet in Person

A family meeting should be in person, but don't hold it over a holiday—it's not something to cram in around a Thanksgiving dinner or a wedding. Dedicate the necessary time to have the conversations you want to have. Your first meeting should be a few hours long. I suggest people gather someplace enjoyable for the weekend. Go on a trip together. Have a barbecue after you meet. Do something afterward where you can simply bond.

Many clients have family members that live out of town, and the family meetings are scheduled in advance, so everyone has the date blocked off on their schedules. Generally, they include some fun stuff after the family meeting. Could be a day or a weekend of family bonding. You can take turns having each family member plan the outing for the next meeting. Again, your family, your rules.

Spend Some Money

Your family may be spread out across the country, and it may be financially difficult for everyone to attend. Maybe somebody needs a babysitter, a pet sitter, or a plane ticket. Be prepared to invest some money to make it happen. You'll be glad you did.

Plan to Meet Again

Don't expect your family meeting to be a one-and-done sort of thing. Once started, they will continue forever. Initially you may meet more often to get the structure and major topics addressed. Schedule in advance for the next year; quarterly or every six months is recommended at this point. You want to make sure the family is aligned and on the same page. Keep the communication and information flowing.

Why People Avoid Family Meetings

Even if you want a family meeting and see the benefits, there may be someone in the family who does not. What do you do?

If someone I am working with is truly resistant to the idea of having a family meeting, I ask, "Why not?" They don't normally have a good answer. I ask them if they understand what a family meeting can do. I make sure they understand the purpose of a family meeting is to align the family and manage and create a plan for the growth and ultimately the disposal of family assets. Again, this is not dinner around the table; this is doing business.

I let them know a proper family meeting brings the family together to help plan for the future of the business and help strengthen the relationships of the business and the family. It opens up the lines of communication between generations and flushes out any conflicts that may need to be addressed.

As often as not, before this process begins, the generation in charge and the generation coming up aren't even talking to each other effectively. If you have a couple of family members working in the business, they tend to have side conversations at family gatherings that no one else understands. This can put a wedge between family members. They feel like they are out of the loop or not the favourite. It can put a strain on sibling relationships.

There are other reasons for avoiding a family meeting. Someone might think, *I see my family all the time, so what's different about a family meeting?* When that happens, go back to the previous answer and explain to them or to yourself what a family meeting is and is not.

Another common reason is to ignore the problem and hope it goes away. But problems, particularly around money, never go away on their own. You might be tempted to stick your head in the sand about entitlement, personalities, skill sets, all kinds of things. Sometimes kids think they already know the answers. A child might assume that they're going to get half the estate when their parents die, not knowing that all the parent's assets are tied up in the business and there is no liquidity, or what that means for their inheritance. Or one sibling might think they will inherit the entire business because they work in it and their brother or sister doesn't. You can imagine how upset people are when they discover that what they "knew" was incorrect. These are important topics to address at a family meeting so that things don't go awry if someone's assumptions turn out to be wrong. Tell them the purpose is to bring clarity around estate planning.

You might also think you don't have enough of an estate for which to plan. This could cause fear that you don't want your kids to look at you differently because you're not as successful as they think you are. Most of us have different relationships with money. It's important to understand each other's attitude toward money so you can come to an understanding. When I grew up, we learned that you didn't talk about politics, sex, religion, or money. Many people grew up in families where their elders didn't talk about money or the value of their estates. It just wasn't done. We tend to talk about those things more now, but many of us still don't talk about finances with our kids. It is a hard conversation to start, and we feel it is none of their business. *I am the parent. I shouldn't have to answer to them.* I am not suggesting you talk about the nitty-gritty details; I am talking about a fifty thousand–foot, aerial-view approach, an overview of estate assets. Just do it. You are reading this book, so something is telling you to make some changes. One bite at a time.

Another reason for avoiding a family meeting might be that you just don't know how to start the conversation. If you are from the generation of people who never had any of the "talks" with their parents, how would you know how to talk about money now? You probably don't. You may be uncomfortable with the topic. But talking about money is essential if you are going to have good family relationships that aren't undermined by assumptions, guesses, questions, or resentments. Stop with the excuses and get started. Get the help you need to get these conversations going.

What is the Desired Outcome?

A good outcome is when family members understand the value of problem-solving and finding solutions together as a family. They have open and honest communications. And everyone feels heard and respected.

Many of the families I work with are pleasantly surprised by this process. They didn't understand the three circles or hadn't really thought about the ownership options available to them. They didn't recognize the many choices and opportunities they had. People tell me they are grateful to feel heard. They are glad they have been educated. They are glad they understand why the business and the family do the things that they do, such as donating regularly to a charity.

Many people tell me they didn't understand the level of control they have over their futures. They say they do things "because that's the way we do it," without thinking about why. But after good family meetings, they know why they do what they do—and they may decide to make changes. They can do so with greater understanding.

Family meetings build cohesion and create opportunities for development. The meetings bring everyone together for a shared purpose, and they are an opportunity to explore what family members want and help them get it.

The first gen may want to stop working. The next generation may want to get into the business but feel they haven't been asked or don't yet have the skills they need. Good family meetings help everyone understand each other better, why the family is doing what it is doing, and how to move forward together.

Be curious at your family meetings. Ask the questions you always wanted to ask but never felt you had the opportunity. Family meetings get the communication flowing!

Use the Family Meeting Agenda on the next page as a starting point for your family meeting. More agenda templates can be found on our website, *www.blueroots.ca*.

FAMILY MEETING AGENDA

Date   _____

Location   _____

Time   _____

Facilitator   (ex. Trusted Advisor)

Purpose   To open the lines of communication for the Family and Business

Participants   All Family Members

Agenda Items & Time Spent

5 mins	POSITIVE FOCUS
5 mins	Expectations for Meeting
10 mins	Ground Rules for Meeting (ex. no phones)
10 mins	Understanding Purpose of Family Meetings
10 mins	Each Member's Perspective of Business
10 mins	Understanding Succession Planning for Business
5 mins	Summary of Business Current Situation
5 mins	Setting Future Family Business Meetings (ex. every 3 months)

Next Steps

_____

_____

_____

Date for Next Meeting

(3 months between meetings)

SUCCESS QUESTIONS

If you are facilitating your own meetings, have your family members bring their answers to the first meeting and have a roundtable discussion on each question below. With these answers you will create your future Family Meeting Agenda.

Sample family circle questions:

- How does communication work in your family?
  - Does it work as it is now?
  - How would you like it to change?

- How are family decisions made?

- How are conflicts resolved?

- Where do you see yourself in the family hierarchy? What role do you play?
  - What are the roles of your other family members?

- What keeps you up at night?

- Are you interested in joining the family business or taking on a bigger role?

- Where do you see yourself in five years?

- Do you understand your family's priorities for the use of the family wealth?

- Do you feel heard in a family setting?

Sample business circle questions:

- What role would you like in the family business, if any?
    - Do you feel you would need more education or training before taking on that role?

- Do you know what the plans are for the business in five to ten years?

- Is the business essential to the family's financial future?
    - Or do you not know?

- Do you understand the impact of the business in the community?
    - Are you proud of it, and why or why not?

- Are you proud of the family business, and why or why not?

Sample ownership circle questions:

- Are you interested in becoming an owner in the future?

- Do you feel the upcoming generation has the skill set to become owners?
    - Do you feel you have the skill set to be an owner?

- Would you like to see the business remain in the family?

- Would ownership fit into your overall financial goals?

- Do you understand the types of ownership options available?

You should choose around ten questions in total to ask each family member for the first meeting.

If you are looking to ask key employees some questions, you may want the questions to revolve around clarity of roles, communication, and the future of the business in the event of uncertainty.

It may be harder to get an open and honest answer if you are the boss to anyone attending the meeting who is answering questions. They might answer the way they think you want them to answer. Using a third party to ask the questions and summarize the answers for you may be the best option.

CHAPTER 7

START PREPARING YOUR BUSINESS FOR SUCCESSION TODAY

"Before anything else, preparation is the key to success."
—ALEXANDER GRAHAM BELL, Scottish-born inventor, scientist,
    and engineer

Having a business that is in tip-top shape is essential whether you are planning to sell or transition it to the next generation. Or, in many cases, when an unexpected transition occurs due to a death or disability.

Imagine what your life would be like if you didn't have to worry about every single aspect of running your business. What if it was someone else's job to be concerned with day-to-day issues? What if payroll, customer service, paperwork, or any other part of your job you dislike was never your problem again, because someone you trust was on top of it? Think about what you could devote your time to instead.

If you can't imagine that . . . well, you're not the only one! For too many family business owners, such a vision seems out of reach. But it doesn't have to.

Business problems fall into four main categories: the people, the processes, the vision, and the values. Get these right and you will be well on your way to having a business that will be easy to transition or sell. Or just maybe, once you get your business prepared, you will want to stay on in a different capacity or ownership type.

If you're going to pass the business down to the next generation, you want to give them a fighting chance for success by making sure it is running smoothly before they take over.

No one knows the issues or problems better than you do. You have been there from the beginning. You also know that the next generation won't get better by themselves. It is going to take some time and dedication to identify what needs to be worked on.

You must take the time to prepare a list of what needs improvement and prioritize that list based on urgency. It doesn't mean you have to make the changes and improvements yourself. You can recruit your current staff to help or seek to outsource the talent you need. We will talk more about this throughout the chapter. As an owner you have the work of strategic thinking and making key decisions in addition to your daily work as an employee in the business.

Regardless of which path you want to take, ensuring your business is self-reliant is the key to moving forward. To make that happen, you need the right policies and procedures in place and the right people around you. Your business must work properly without you to be of maximum value to your successor or to a buyer. That value lies in setting it up to be a self-reliant operation—which means going through a process to understand your obstacles and remove them.

Outsourcing

What initially made you successful may be very different from what you need to keep your business growing and running successfully. Different skills are required. You started in your trade, you did a great job, earned a good reputation in your industry, and before long you realized you had a family business.

It is important to understand what you're good at, the skill sets that are required to move a business forward, and what you like to do. If you're like a lot of our clients, you might not have as firm a grasp of those things as you need. You're bogged down with administrative work and managing employees. Your to-do list dominates your life. You are further and further away from what you love to do.

For instance, you probably are not that excited about accounting and bookkeeping. Many clients we work with who are on the smaller side may go months without sending their invoices out. They fall far behind in their bookkeeping and invoicing because they don't like to do it or aren't good at it. They don't even know where they stand financially. Outsourcing is a great way to redistribute the workload and not have to hire a full-time position. You can hire someone to do your books part time, as often as needed. One day a week or one day a month! They are professionals that you don't have to train, and they are a productive part of your team immediately. Even better if the referral came from your accountant!

We have been outsourcing for many years, starting when we realized we didn't have the skill set internally but didn't need a full-time role. I was skeptical at first but decided to be open and try it. We are frequent users of outsourcing now.

I asked one of my clients the other day about the value of their business, and they said, "It would be worth more if we sent out our invoices and collected the money. We are so busy doing the work we don't have time!" This is a big indicator that you need to outsource some of the things you either aren't good at, don't have the skill sets for, or just plain don't like doing.

There are many areas that you can outsource, like human resources and marketing. You probably need the help but not full time. Just think about how great it would be to hand some of those tasks off to someone else. How much happier and more productive you would be. Ask your advisors for referrals or recommendations.

Establish Processes

When you start out, you may have one or two employees, maybe a buddy or a cousin who comes in to help, and then stays with the business. Everybody knows what needs to be done and does it. As you grow, things get complicated. What is the role for a new employee? What is the pay rate? Do you have the right compensation model? What is your hourly rate to your clients, and how does that have to change when you have employees?

Processes quickly become important. If you don't have a process for compensation, for instance, you are reinventing the wheel every time you hire someone. How do you decide what to pay them, what benefits they are eligible for, whether you are covering the cost of their truck? How do you develop your people? What is the process if someone wants to step into a manager role? Do you say, "OK, you're the manager," or do you have internal transition plans? If you're not consistent, you can get in trouble before you know it. Employees talk. You must be transparent as you grow your company. You don't want people talking behind your back.

Writing processes probably isn't something you want to be doing, and it may not be something you enjoy doing. However, it is very important if you want growth, to transition, or to sell at some point in the future. If writing isn't your strong suit, you can start recording your thoughts or use AI programs to record meetings and send you the transcripts when complete. The thoughts or meeting notes can then be sent to the correct person or department to set up a task for you, like to prepare the invoice or client proposal. Some people love taking notes and documenting. I am not one of them, but I must do it, and how to make it less painful is my ultimate goal.

If it all seems overwhelming, remember how to eat an elephant— one bite at a time. Take it slow, make a list of issues that need to be looked at, and rank them. Start with number one. If you are not sure how to get started, call someone. You have your trusted advisors, industry associations, and other businesses you know that you can ask. Regardless of the business you are in, we all suffer or have suffered from the same issues over the growth of our businesses.

Is Your Target Market Defined?

You can't be all things to all people. You have to define who you want to work with—who do you do your best work for, or who is the most profitable? They are not always the same. This is your target market, and you define it. Once you understand who they are, and who you do the best work for, you can focus your time and energy on those clients and potential clients. Then you aren't wasting any time, effort, or money attracting the wrong target market. If you want to deal only with commercial clients, don't accept residential clients or the word will spread.

Make sure everybody on your team understands who your clients are and why. Pick a lane and stick to it. I know it is hard to do, and you may have to walk away from some business. But it will help the company maintain profitability in the long run; it won't be pulled in all directions trying to be everything to everyone. Are you a trucking service within the province or a delivery service within a 100-kilometer radius of your town? Pick a lane.

Having your target market defined will make it easier to make that differentiation.

For example, our target market is small (under one hundred employees), first-generation, family-run businesses. They are looking to prepare their families and businesses for a transition. They want to strengthen their relationship and open communication to make the best decisions for both the family and the business.

What Differentiates You from Your Competitor?

What's your elevator pitch? You should be able to tell me in a couple of words or sentences why I should deal with you instead of your competitor. What makes you better? Is it twenty-four-hour service? Is it quick response time? Is it that you can solve any problem? If you can't put your finger on what differentiates you, you may have a problem.

Take a look at what your competitors are doing. Are they a threat to your business? Are they doing things better than you are? Is their reputation better than yours? Or do you see them as an opportunity because you know you are better on several levels, and you just need to get the word out?

Are Your Office Processes Written Down?

No one can read your mind. If you are thinking about succession or transition, or selling, the stronger the systems and processes, the easier it is to transition or the more valuable the business is to the buying party. The more the business can survive without you, the more valuable the business is.

What if a potential client calls and your salesperson is unavailable? Does the person answering the phone know what to do? Do they know how to set the right expectation about when someone will call them back? If someone goes out on a sales call or answers the phone, you want to be confident that they are going to deliver a consistent message: *This is what we do, this is how we do it, this is the result.*

When you started out you probably had to do everything yourself, so you may not have needed to write your processes down, but as you grew, documentation became more and more important. You, as the owner, have the company and systems in your head. But you can't keep it there. You need to document processes throughout the business. If you don't want to do this yourself, get someone to follow you around with a notebook and describe what you do so they can write it down. You may have to get very detailed: "I open up our database, I go to this file, I click on this tab . . ."

Getting this information out of your head frees you to think about more important things and empowers the people around you to do their jobs. You may not like writing processes, but someone in your business or family probably does. Back again to communication. If you don't mention it, how will you know if your bookkeeper or daughter-in-law loves that stuff?

Having processes written down serves many purposes. What if someone is sick and another on holiday—can anyone fill in when needed for a couple of hours? Do they know where to go for the answers? Hiring is also much easier when you have documented processes. The further away we get from the day-to-day operations, the harder it is to step in when needed. If the processes are documented, anyone can step in in a pinch.

Do You Have an Organizational Chart that Includes Roles and Responsibilities?

Having written job descriptions and duties may sound basic, but I can't tell you how many businesses don't have them. They rely on a job posting as their description of role and responsibilities.

I had a client with twenty-five employees and ten million in revenue without documented roles and responsibilities. What a shocker when they finally got them done. They realized they had too many people touching the same file, costing them valuable time and money. The streamlining was a game changer for the transition. In fact, generation two was involved in gathering the information. What a great way to get a full understanding of the roles in family business.

If you don't have a clear understanding of the roles and responsibilities in your company, start by asking individuals to write down what they do every day, for a week. You might learn something. For instance, you might think you need to hire another salesperson, but when you look at what your existing salesperson does, you realize they don't need to be doing half of what's on their plate. You see that a lot of their tasks can be handed off to an administrative assistant—that's who you need, not another salesperson.

It can be hard to figure out what someone is worth until you know what they do. If your salesperson is spending half their time invoicing and half their time selling, then they are not worth as much as if they are spending all of their time selling.

As you grow, you need to know what you're hiring for and understand the cost and value of the hire. If you send an electrician out on a job, you can bill the client for their time. But if you hire an administrative assistant, you can't directly bill a client for that person's time. Understand how hires change your costs, and you may have to change the way you price your work.

If you don't have an accountability chart, organizational chart, or whatever you want to call it—anything where you can see the roles in the business—or you haven't updated it in the last two years, this is where you need to start. If service is your focus, you may realize that you need more service team members.

When doing this exercise, make sure you take the name of the person currently doing the role out of the chart. Complete the title, duties, and responsibilities of that role, not what the person currently in that role does. Sometimes the role is not a full-time role, or it's too much for one person, and that's OK. You will figure it out once the chart is complete. You may realize you have one person in two roles for now. That's OK. Break the role into what it should look like. Really look at duties and responsibilities of the role. I like to see the chart expanded to what I want it to be a few years from now; others like to shorten it to a year or two. Either way is fine. As Nike says, *just do it*.

Having your chart readily available and up-to-date makes it easier for family members and employees to understand the current and future roles in the business plus the possible opportunities.

If you feel overwhelmed by all of this, as I sure did, you can hire someone to come in and help. There is lots of help available out there. Don't push it off because it is not your strong suit. I did that for many years. Finally giving in to outside help—another one of the best things ever!

Leverage the talents of others and ask the advisors you deal with for recommendations. If you need a bookkeeper, ask your accountant for a recommendation. If you need help with HR, ask other family business owners who they use as an outside firm. If you are part of an association, ask your fellow members for a name.

There are groups and associations specifically for family-run businesses. They are a great resource for all family and business issues. Look up and join your local family business association; there are organizations worldwide.

Is Everyone in the Right Role?

When you start hiring, not every role will be full time, so you need to have someone who is adaptable, can juggle a few roles and responsibilities, may not be the best at everything but can manage. But as you grow, you'll notice that sometimes things are not done quite right, or they're not done on time. When that happens, look at the individual and the role and ask, is that a capacity issue? Are they doing too much? Are we growing and they don't have the time to do the work? Or is it that they don't have the capability to do the work? Are they now in over their head? For instance, do they have the title of general manager but the skill set of an operations manager? Is it that they can't do the job, or that they don't know how to do the job? Did I just keep giving them more and more to do until they were in over their head?

To give your employees a fighting chance, you both must understand what their role is, what their responsibilities are, and what their capabilities are. Use the information from the "What do you do every day?" exercise. You may think you know, but do you? This ties into documenting roles and responsibilities. As your company grows and changes, so do the roles. Revisit these every few years or after a big change in the business.

You may trust and respect the people in your business; however, that is not reason enough to promote them. I have seen people elevated into the wrong role because of who they are or their length of service, and not necessarily based on their skill set. A good example is moving your best salesperson into the role of sales manager because they are really good at sales. That might seem logical, but being a good sales manager requires a different skill set from being a good salesperson. You might end up with a weaker sales team and a veteran employee who is miserable. Look at the chart of roles and responsibilities. Are they the right person for the role?

You can avoid some noses getting out of joint by having open, honest discussions about roles and where someone might be able to excel. Promoting them may not always be the best thing to do, but having respect for them and what they contribute is essential for every role. Only promote when they have the capability, understand the role, and actually want the role. It will help build a stronger team and a stronger business if you have the right people in the right roles.

Don't forget to give positive feedback when you see the opportunity to do so. We tend to want to talk about what is wrong, but if you say, "Oh, nice job," or "Thanks for cleaning up my coffee cup," or "You did great work on that case," it goes a long way. No appreciation is too small. This kind of supportive feedback builds a team, regardless of where they sit on the chart. You run a family business, and when you treat your employees like family, they become part of the family. You know their spouse's names and their kids' sports teams. You care for each other. That gets lost in a big company. It's a real advantage of a family business, so don't lose sight of it. It is one of your family's advantages.

> **Important Note:** Do family members get a different salary for a role just because they are family members? My son got the same salary as anybody else in his role would have received. I was trying to set him up for success in the business, not set him up for silver spoon comments behind his back.

Be mindful of overcompensating family members and what it can do to their reputation and credibility, not to mention to the office culture. Remember the three circles—family members will get perks; however, in the business, they are employees.

Is Your Leadership Team Truly Open and Honest in Your Meetings?

Can your leadership team have hard conversations with you and each other? Do they challenge you or just go along with your ideas? Hard conversations can be stressful, but they are necessary for the success of your business. Hard conversations are a part of the leadership role.

The best way to build a stronger team and business is to be open and honest with each other. This doesn't mean picking on people, but it is about being able to talk to someone about an issue when it comes up to help them and the company succeed.

Everyone at some point needs some guidance or clarification; if you can't be open and honest with each other about what is working and what isn't, you're not going to make progress as a leader and a company.

Bring conversations back to values and goals. If your leadership team knows what you're trying to do, they can help you and the company succeed. Be open to hearing other points of view. The more perspectives you have, the better the solution is going to be. If you have a "my way or the highway" approach, you're not likely to keep your good people for long, and you're not likely to succeed. If your team members don't feel heard or feel like they will be wasting their time bringing up an opposing position, it will only hurt the business and any future plans you may have.

Take Time Each Week to Work ON the Business

"*On* the business, *in* the business." It took me quite a while to truly understand what that meant. *In* is pretty easy. You are doing your regular job, you are working in the business. Working *on* is what this book is about. Looking at strategy, development, vision, everything in this book is focused on *on* the business, on the bigger picture. If you haven't worked *on* the business because "I don't have time," you have a problem. However, you are reading this, so that is promising!

When you're an owner who also works in the business, the line between owner and employee can get blurry. There are many blurred lines in a family business. When you come to work and tackle your to-do list, you are behaving like an employee. You are compensated like an employee for that, and you play by the same rules as an employee when you do that. But as the owner you are more than an employee, and you must make space to put on the other hats and work *on* the business as well.

Go back and look at the organizational chart. If your name is in every role, you are doing too much, and things are going to get worse, not better. If you had an employee in that situation, you would intervene. You would ask, "Do you need some help, someone to take things off your plate?"

Why not do the same thing for yourself? You have a responsibility to be the captain of the ship. You can't be up in the rig hanging the sails or down in the bilge manning the pumps. You must steer. Schedule time to work on the business, and make sure your team knows that time is not an opportunity to interrupt you. It is your thinking time. It's probably not hard for you to come up with things you'd like to see happen with the business. Write them down, maybe bounce some ideas off your family or leadership team. Once you have a list, ask yourself, *What's the most important thing here that I need to accomplish?* Then do that one thing. You might decide, *I'm going to find somebody to help me write my job descriptions*, or *I'm going to get a facilitator to help our team work on our core values*. Remember the elephant—take it in small bites. Don't spin your wheels reorganizing your list; figure out the most important thing and get started. Don't keep putting it off. Schedule the time and make it happen.

You might say, well, I don't need to work on it, everything seems fine. But it's only fine until it's not, and it's a lot harder to fix something after it breaks than to deal with it before it becomes a crisis. The best way to deal with a crisis is to head it off or have a solution ready ahead of time. When you were starting your business, you didn't have to worry about this. Now you have a growing business, family depending on you, employees depending on you, and you need to spend time focusing *on* the business. You have an obligation to spend time on it. It is a top priority; it is part of the ownership role.

I know it is hard to set aside the time to work on the business when you are busy working in the business. However, when you are pressed for time is the best time to work on the business. It means you are stretched too thin, and something will have to give. The crisis will be just around the corner if you don't take a step back and look at the big picture. I book my *on the business* time in my calendar in advance. I block off one to two days every quarter. Part of the time is alone, and part of the time is with others so I can debrief them and get all my ideas out and get some feedback. You can use family, your leadership team, anyone you want; your business, your choice. Then delegate and get the success train moving. Get those new ideas implemented.

Family businesses often consume their owners to the point where they ignore their families and don't have much life outside of work. As an owner, if you set that example, you can be certain that your key employees will follow your lead. You might think that's a good thing—everybody is working hard because you're working hard—but it's not a recipe for a smooth succession. To begin, you need to develop boundaries around work because giving yourself down time, a chance to recharge, gives you space to think. Second, if you run people ragged you won't keep them. You'll lose key employees. Those employees are an important part of a succession plan. They should want to stay after you step back. Create a culture that doesn't burn people out and that respects your commitments to your family as well as your commitments to your business.

Working all the time may deter your family from wanting to join the family business. Based on my experience, the majority of my first-generation owners struggle with wanting their kids to come into the business. They have no downtime, and they want better for their family. Avoid this trap; work smarter, not harder, as they say.

Do You Delegate Responsibilities?

If you're swamped every day, if you feel you "don't have time to do anything," try to delegate just a little bit. You'll realize that not only do you free up time to do the things you love to do, and to do the things you need to do (like spend quality time working on the business), but you've also given somebody else an opportunity to step up and shine. For instance, you don't have to hand over all your accounting. But maybe you can ask someone to do the invoicing.

When you delegate, you elevate. You lift someone to a new level with new responsibilities. People feel good about that. They feel important. They become a more important part of the team, and they take a load off your shoulders—not only in terms of doing the invoicing, but also being the person who handles all the invoicing questions.

The hardest thing about delegating is micromanaging. Don't do it! Show them how to do the job and let them do it. That's not easy to do when you've been doing it yourself for so long, but it's necessary. I know it is quicker to do it yourself than to teach someone to do it, but it will be worth it in the long run; it will free up your time. Make sure you go back and look at your organizational charts, roles and responsibilities. Who is best suited to take on this new task? Do they have the time and the skill set? Make sure you are not piling it on to a person who is already at capacity. You may be overwhelming them or putting them in a situation they are not really qualified for. Once a decision has been made to delegate (or outsource), add the task to the chart.

Is Your Compensation Package Competitive?

When you have a family-run business, your employees are not generally there because they want to climb the corporate ladder. They have a different career path in mind. They like the respect and appreciation they get, the flexibility that a small company can provide, the closeness of their team, and the satisfaction they get from the work they do.

To stay competitive and attract the right people, make sure they are compensated fairly. If you're not sure, do a little research or delegate the task. If there is a relevant union in your industry, check with them. See if you can find out what your competitors pay. Spend a little time on Google. Although you don't have a ladder for employees to climb, you can be attractive in many other ways. If they don't have much prospect for advancement, think about how to compensate them in other ways.

There are many ways to compensate, such as company-wide bonuses, a company car, retirement contributions, health and dental benefits, flex hours, or work-from-home flexibility. Perhaps you can simply stock the kitchen with things they like to eat. You still need to be competitive in salary, but you may be able to offer things that other companies can't.

Your goal is to have people who are happy to be there and who love what you are offering. Google will tell you what fair base pay is. It's the other things you can offer that will make them want to stay, including your values and your culture. Experienced employees are very valuable—don't lose them over a couple of dollars.

Ensure you have each employee's compensation package documented, including perks; this will make it easier for everyone, particularly while planning a transition. Make sure there are no verbal agreements that can come back and bite either party.

SUCCESS QUESTIONS

The following questions are to get you thinking about starting your succession planning today. Not every question will be relevant to you—that's OK. Focus on the ones that matter. This will help you to break down your business and understand where you need help most. Use the space provided or grab a sheet of paper. Don't skip it.

As you read each one, think of someone asking you the question. What is the first answer that comes to mind? Write it down.

- Is there something on your list that you need help with and could outsource?

- Is your target market defined?

- What differentiates you from your competitor?

- Are your office processes written down?

- Do you have an organizational chart that includes roles and responsibilities?

- Is everyone in the right role?

- Is your leadership team truly open and honest, or do they just go along with anything you say?

- As the business owner, do you take time each week to work *on* the business?

- Do you delegate responsibilities?

- Is your compensation package competitive?

CONCLUSION

"If you don't think you can do it, who will?
You control the most important tool in success, your mind."
—Jeffrey Gitomer, American author, salesperson, and speaker

suc·cess
Noun the accomplishment of an aim or purpose.

You are well on your way to preparing your family and business to pass on your success. Family business succession is challenging, especially when it is the first generation figuring out what to do. I hope by now you have a better understanding of where you should focus your efforts as you address the issues that are unique to your family and your business.

In Chapter 1, we talked about knowing what you want and how to get there. It's not as easy as it sounds. Particularly in a family business, you must know what everybody wants, needs, and expects. A shared view of what today, tomorrow, and an eventual succession plan looks like is key.

In Chapter 2, we went over that to achieve success you must visualize and communicate what you want: what you want for yourself, for the future of your business, for your family, for your legacy. You can only get where you are going if you choose to go there. Communication is the key to success!

We also discussed, in that same chapter, the power of viewing the stakeholders in your family business as members of one or more circles: family, business, owner. Each one has a different perspective. Sometimes a stakeholder sits in more than one circle. Understanding someone's perspective means understanding where they sit. Understand yourself too. When you approach a decision or react to a situation, ask yourself which hat you are wearing.

In Chapter 3, we analyzed the business circle of the Family Business Model. This is where you learned about the importance of clearly established and written vision, values, and goals. If you weren't sure how to develop values beforehand, you read about a great exercise to establish them.

In Chapter 4, you learned about the ownership circle. Here, you learned about the three types of ownership and how to begin talking about the possibilities of family succession.

In Chapter 5, we dove into perhaps the most important circle of the three—family. Specifically, we discussed the most common challenges of a family business and how to deal with them. Fears, money discomfort, sibling rivalries, and many other issues exist within the unique dynamic that is the family business. To successfully navigate these waters, you will need to pay particularly close attention to the information found here.

In Chapter 6, you learned the importance of the family meeting. It is not a mythical creature as some would suggest. It is a real thing and imperative to running, growing, and potentially passing on your business someday. Keep this chapter bookmarked, as you may want to use it as reference for how to hold a family meeting and what the desired outcome should look like.

In Chapter 7, you read about a variety of tasks that must be completed and updated on a regular basis to ensure the ability to execute a smooth succession. That day could be in a few months, a few years, or many years down the road. It doesn't matter. Succession planning should be a part of running your daily to-do list.

Throughout the book, some common themes emerged. You learned about why growth is likely going to be necessary for an effective succession, and I introduced you to some key topics to consider as you prepare your company for growth and for its own life without you. By spending time on operations, you lay the foundation for a self-managing business. Even if you plan to work in your business for many years, you will be glad you have done this.

I also shared some thoughts on asking for help and who to ask. Building a business is a challenge. Running a business is a challenge. Nurturing a family is a challenge. Passing a business on is a challenge. Put all of them together, and you have a complex stew that is unique in the business world. Who could possibly be expected to do all of those things well without help? Seek advisors, be discerning in who you bring in, and make the most of the help you can get.

The success questions at the end of each chapter are there to help you start thinking and better understanding your family and your business issues. You should by now have a better grip on all the issues that you face. If you are like most people, you read things that you never have thought about. Good! Now you know what you need to take care of. That is one less unpleasant surprise for you or someone else in the future. You should have a sense of the areas in your business and your family that need the most focused attention. Optimally, you know where to start. The important thing is to start somewhere.

Finally, thank you for reading this book. As I said in the opening pages, I think it is a tragedy that so many good family businesses don't succeed beyond the first generation. You have taken a step toward changing that, and that makes me incredibly happy. By having a robust succession plan in place, you will realize the best value out of your family business, whether another generation succeeds you, you keep it and hire someone to run it for you, or you sell it. No matter your desire, you can set up a plan that will make that desire a success thanks to strong family dynamics, clear values, an understanding of where you are going, the right people around you or the new owner, and trusted advisors.

Remember, I am here to help. You can access some free resources on my website, *www.blueroots.ca*, or send me an email at *tammy@blueroots.ca*.

It is never too late to start your succession journey, and I am here to help you pass on your success.

APPENDIX

Help
Verb make it easier for (someone) to do something by offering one's services or resources.

If there's one nugget I want you to take from this book, it's to start your succession planning now.

The second you find this all too much and overwhelming, ask for help. Don't just put this book down and forget about it.

There are professionals that can help you with systems, processes, succession planning, and family communication, just to name a few.

You are probably already working with several who can help you, but they are not working together on your issue. The key to a successful plan is to have a lead or project manager who can keep the project moving forward and coordinate with all the other parties to get your project completed.

Key Success Advisors
- CPA (Certified Public Accountant): to help you strategize the best tax planning for the business and the family.

- Lawyer: specializing in business, to help you with business needs, wills, POAs and trusts.

- CLU (Chartered Life Underwriter): an advisor specializing in life insurance for the business and the family.

- CFP (Certified Financial Planner) or CFA (Chartered Financial Analyst): a wealth manager who can help with a financial plan and manage family and business financial assets

- FEA (Family Enterprise Advisor): an advisor who can facilitate family meetings and provide unbiased advice; generally the center of the hub that pulls all the parties together and takes a leading role in the collaboration process.

- TEP (Trust and Estate Practitioner): specialist in inheritance and succession planning; valuable when building an estate plan.

Key advisors may carry more than one designation, and that is great. They look through different lenses when presented with an issue, and if they share a designation, they understand each other a little better. Regardless of how many you have, it is important that you have all the bases covered and the advisors know each other and can collaborate to come up with the best solution for your business and your family when an issue comes up—preferably before it comes up. They may have differing opinions on a particular subject depending on their discipline, but by working together they will come up with the best solution for you.

Build your team, make your life easier.

They will also be a valuable resource for referrals as needed—bookkeepers, HR specialists, and whatever else your family needs—one of the advisors will know someone.

Tammy Buss

TAMMY BUSS *has helped hundreds of Canadian family businesses during her thirty-year career. The founder of Buss Financial Group, Buss Business Solutions and BlueRoots Inc, she has navigated the very issues she writes about. Through her client experience and trial-and-error in her own family, she has developed and refined successful business transition strategies and tactics. She is a Certified Financial Planner, Chartered Life Underwriter, Chartered Financial Consultant, and Family Enterprise Advisor.*

www.ingramcontent.com/pod-product-compliance
Lightning Source LLC
Chambersburg PA
CBHW071712210326
41597CB00017B/2457